## BASIC / NOT BORING
## SCIENCE SKILLS

# HUMAN BODY
# & HEALTH

## Grades 6–8⁺

Inventive Exercises to Sharpen
Skills and Raise Achievement

Series Concept & Development
by Imogene Forte & Marjorie Frank
Exercises by Marjorie Frank

Incentive Publications, Inc.
Nashville, Tennessee

*About the cover:*
Bound resist, or tie dye, is the most ancient known method of fabric surface design. The brilliance of the basic tie dye design on this cover reflects the possibilities that emerge from the mastery of basic skills.

*Illustrated by Kathleen Bullock*
*Cover art by Mary Patricia Deprez, dba Tye Dye Mary®*
*Cover design by Marta Drayton, Joe Shibley, and W. Paul Nance*
*Edited by Jean K. Signor*

ISBN 0-86530-552-8

PRINTED IN THE UNITED STATES OF AMERICA
www.incentivepublications.com

# TABLE OF CONTENTS

# CELEBRATE BASIC SCIENCE SKILLS

Basic does not mean boring! There certainly is nothing dull about . . .
   . . . snooping around the body like a detective to solve body mysteries
   . . . watching body parts search the classified ads for jobs
   . . . tracking down body organs and designer genes
   . . . learning about the talents of periosteum, pectorals, the pancreas, and the patella
   . . . visiting the Broken Bones Clinic to figure out which bones are fractured
   . . . figuring out how patients taste and smell hospital food
   . . . searching for a safety pin lost in someone's digestive system
   . . . sympathizing with 30 different complaining patients in an emergency room
   . . . looking over the shoulder to see if first aid students are making good first decisions

The idea of celebrating the basics is just what it sounds like—enjoying and getting good at knowing all about the parts of the body and the way they function. Each page invites learners to try a high-interest, appealing exercise that will sharpen or review one specific science skill, concept, or process. This is not just another ordinary fill-in-the-blanks way to learn. These exercises are fun and surprising. Students will do the useful work of deepening science knowledge while they follow dozens of delightful doctors, patients, and workers around a Medical Center. These quirky characters will lead them to explore and deepen their understanding of the functioning of the body and the basics of health and fitness.

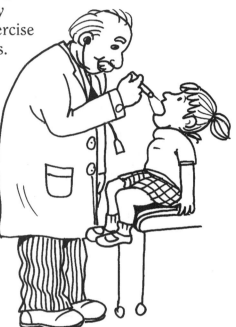

The pages in this book can be used in many ways:
- for individual students to sharpen a particular skill
- with a small group needing to relearn or strengthen a skill
- as an instructional tool for teaching a skill to any size group
- by students working on their own
- by students working under the direction of an adult

**Each page may be used to introduce a new skill, to reinforce a skill, or even to assess a student's performance of a skill.** And, there's more than just the great student activities! You will also find an appendix of resources helpful for students and teachers—including a ready-to-use test for assessing skills and understandings about the body.

The pages are written with the assumption that an adult will be available to assist the student with their learning and practice. It will also be helpful for students to have access to science resources such as a science textbook, encyclopedias, and Internet reference sources.

As your students take on the challenges of these adventures with the human body and health, they will grow. As you watch them check off the basic science skills they have sharpened, you can celebrate with them!

**The Skills Test** (pages 56–59)
   Use the skills test as a pretest and/or a post-test. This will help you check the students' mastery of basic skills and understandings related to the human body and health. It can also prepare them for success on tests of standards, instructional goals, or other individual achievement.

# SKILLS CHECKLIST FOR HUMAN BODY & HEALTH

| ✔ | SKILL | PAGE(S) |
|---|---|---|
| | Identify different body processes, body activities, and body parts | 10–13 |
| | Identify some parts of the human cell and their functions | 14 |
| | Identify different types of cells | 15 |
| | Distinguish between cells, tissue, organs and systems; name different kinds of tissue, organs, and systems | 15 |
| | Identify functions of different body systems; distinguish among systems | 16–17 |
| | Identify specific organs within systems | 17 |
| | Identify bones in the skeletal system and functioning of the skeletal system | 18–21 |
| | Identify joints, ligaments, cartilage, and their functions | 20 |
| | Identify muscles and understand functioning of the muscular system | 21 |
| | Identify parts of the nervous system and understand functioning of the system | 22–23 |
| | Identify different parts of the brain and their functions | 22–23 |
| | Show understanding of the function of sensory organs | 24–27 |
| | Identify the parts of the eye and the way the eye sees objects | 24 |
| | Identify parts of the ear and the way they help in hearing | 25 |
| | Show understanding of the way the nose and tongue work to enable the sensations of taste and smell | 26 |
| | Identify parts of the skin and show understanding of the functions of the skin | 27 |
| | Identify parts of the circulatory system and understand functioning of the system | 28–29 |
| | Show understanding of the workings of the heart | 29 |
| | Identify parts of the respiratory system and understand functioning of the system | 30–31 |
| | Identify parts of the digestive system and understand functioning of the system | 32–33 |
| | Identify glands of the endocrine system and understand their functions | 34 |
| | Identify organs that are part of the excretory system and understand their functions | 35 |
| | Identify parts of the male and female reproductive systems and understand functioning of the systems | 36 |
| | Show understanding of the process of fertilization and of the process by which a fertilized egg develops into a human offspring | 36–37 |
| | Show a basic understanding of some concepts of genetics and heredity | 38–39 |
| | Identify different diseases and disorders and their symptoms and causes | 40–41 |
| | Show understanding of some treatments available for different medical problems | 42–43 |
| | Identify the ways bodies can defend against disease, including natural defenses and other interventions | 44–45 |
| | Show understanding of the ways exercise is beneficial to health | 46–47 |
| | Show understanding of nutrition concepts and components of a healthy diet | 48–49 |
| | Show understanding of some basic first aid procedures | 50–51 |
| | Show ability to apply fitness and health concepts to personal life | 52 |

# HUMAN BODY & HEALTH

## Skills Exercises

Entering CITY
MEDICAL CENTER

# BODY MYSTERIES

Students at the Body-Wise Medical Center learn about mysteries of the human body. These 22 mysteries are part of a study guide they are using to prepare for a test. Use your clever thinking, good resources, and knowledge of the human body to track down the solutions to these mysteries.

**1.** Dr. Neuron is standing on her head. Amazingly, when she eats a cookie, it goes through her esophagus into her stomach. What process keeps the food from sliding back up into her mouth as she stands on her head?

_____

**2.** A green substance is lurking in the gallbladder. What is this substance?

_____

**3.** Several small white structures are lodged in sockets in the maxillae and the mandible. What are these structures?

_____

**4.** Some reactions are having a great time leaping across synapses. What are these reactions?

_____

**5.** A liquid is always flowing through the kidneys, being filtered by a million tiny filtering units called nephrons. What is the flowing substance?

_____

**6.** A mysterious substance is frequently coming out of the Islets of Langerhans. What is this substance?

_____

**7.** A substance is getting smashed into tiny pieces in the liver during digestion. What is this substance?

_____

**8.** Red blood cells are busy carrying heavy loads of a substance. What is it?

_____

**9.** A strange reaction is happening inside a body. The diaphragm muscle and muscles in the abdominal wall are strongly contracting. Partly digested food is being forced up out of the stomach. What is happening?

_____

**10.** Dr. Neuron's wrist rotates when she does her jump rope workout. What allows her wrist to rotate?

_____

Use with page 11.

Name _____

*Basic Skills/Human Body & Health 6-8+*

**11.** A fluid called perilymph sloshes around in a coiled tube. What is this tube and where is it located?

_____
_____

**12.** Two substances are mixing together with food in the duodenum. What are these substances?

_____
_____

**13.** A body detective has come across a bunch of cones. What organ is she exploring?

_____

**14.** Tiny structures with great potential make their home in the ovaries. Every month one of them matures and leaves its home. What are these structures?

_____

**15.** A slippery fluid is in the nose. It traps dust particles. What is this fluid?

_____

**16.** A body detective searches for clues in a layer of dentine under a crown. What structure is he exploring?

_____

**17.** A great deal of liquid is passing into the blood through the walls of the colon (the first part of the large intestine). What is this liquid?

_____

**18.** Plasma is busily flowing around the body as a part of the blood. What is plasma carrying?

_____

**19.** Bodies have parts attached to them that have grown out of roots. The visible part is composed of dead cells made hard by a substance called keratin. What are these parts?

_____

**20.** When Dr. Neuron is startled by a terrible crash, her heart pounds. What makes that sound coming from her heart?

_____

**21.** A substance pours into the professor's blood when she hears the crash. This substance prepares her for emergency action such as running away or fighting to protect herself. What is this substance?

_____

**22.** Professor Neuron was so frightened by the noise that she broke the test tube in her hand and sliced two fingers. Amazingly, after a few minutes, the blood clotted and the bleeding stopped. What body structures made this happen?

_____

Use with page 10.

Name _____

# HOT JOBS FOR BODY PARTS

There are plenty of job opportunities for hard-working body parts. Several of the jobs are described here (pages 12 and 13). But which parts are qualified to apply?

Read each job description from the newspaper. Write the name of at least one body part that is qualified and able to do the job. (See the list of possible applicants on page 13.)

## JOBS AVAILABLE

**1. CARRIERS NEEDED**
Carry repeated loads of oxygen-rich blood away from the heart.

_____

**2. HELP WANTED**
Workers needed to separate unwanted substances out of the blood. Please apply in pairs.

_____

**3. WANTED**
Strong applicants to protect human bones. Must have extensive experience in the task of multiplying to grow and repair broken bones.

_____

**4. APPLY TODAY**
Sit a-top the trachea and move muscles to change the shape of vocal cords.

_____

**5. HELP WANTED**
Suck in air and pass it down into the bronchi.

_____

**6. AVAILABLE**
Keep pressure equal on both sides of the eardrum. Must be able to open and close to let air in and out. Please apply in pairs.

_____

**7. WANTED**
Need workers to bend and straighten knees.

_____

**8. APPLY TODAY**
Work with others to raise and lower the forearm.

_____

**9. APPLICANTS NEEDED**
Applicants needed for group work to insulate nerve fibers through an entire body.

_____

**10. WANTED IMMEDIATELY**
Efficient organ needed to produce insulin.

_____

**11. NEEDED**
Tubes needed to carry urine from kidneys to bladder.

_____

**12. COODINATOR**
Experienced worker is needed to balance and coordinate all the body's movements.

_____

**13. WANTED**
Need muscular worker able to move up and down for moving air in and out of the lungs.

_____

**14. JOB OPEN**
Produce hormone to regulate the balance of calcium in the blood and bones.

_____

**15. HIRING NOW**
Workers needed to wrap around harmful bacteria and produce antibodies to combat diseases.

_____

Use with page 13.

Name

## APPLICANTS

alveoli    cerebrum    gall bladder    ovaries    retina    thymus
aorta    cerebellum    humerus    pancreas    sacrum    thyroid
arteries    coccyx    incisors    parathyroid gland    scapula    tongue
appendix    cochlea    iris    patella    semicircular canal    trachea
adrenal glands    cornea    kidneys    periosteum    small intestine    triceps
atrium    dendrites    larynx    pharynx    spinal cord    ureters
biceps    diaphragm    liver    pituitary gland    sternum    urethra
bicuspids    epidermis    marrow    plasma    stomach    uterus
bronchial tubes    epiglottis    medulla    platelets    tear duct    veins
bronchiole    esophagus    molars    pulp    teeth    ventricle
cartilage    Eustachian tube    myelin    quadriceps    tendon    villi
capillaries    Fallopian tube    optic nerve    rectum    testes    white blood cells

## JOBS AVAILABLE

**16. GATEKEEPERS**
Absorb food and pass it into blood vessels from the ileum.

**17. OPPORTUNITY**
Keep many bones from grinding against each other when they move. Rubbery applicants only, please.

**18. APPLY TODAY**
Force food back into pharynx so that it can glide easily down the esophagus.

**19. OPENING**
Light-sensitive worker needed to receive visual images and transmit impulses to the brain.

**20. WANTED**
Worker to help immune system recognize germs and reject them.

**21. JOB AVAILABLE**
Join muscles to bone. Several positions available.

**22. WORKER NEEDED**
Make bile to break up fats during digestion.

**23. APPLY NOW**
Worker needed to produce eleven hormones that control the actions of other endocrine glands.

**24. OPENING**
Regulate heart rate and breathing, swallowing, sneezing, and coughing.

**25. POSITION AVAILABLE**
Take up residence at the end of the vertebrae column. Little activity required for the job.

**26. JOB OPEN**
Keep trachea covered during swallowing.

**27. HELP WANTED**
Workers needed to make blood cells.

**28. WANTED**
Strong workers needed to crush and grind food.

**29. WANTED NOW**
Pair of workers needed to produce estrogen.

**30. OPENINGS**
Workers needed to pass oxygen from lungs into blood vessels and welcome carbon dioxide into the lungs.

*I've got to 'bone up' on my body parts!*

Use with page 12.

Name

# STARTING OUT SIMPLE

Professor Gertrude Golgi is lecturing her
students on the basics of human physiology.
Finish her chart by writing the name of each
cell part that is pictured and described.

*I celebrate the cell.*

The cell is the body's
basic unit of life.
Although there are different kinds of cells,
most of them have a similar structure.

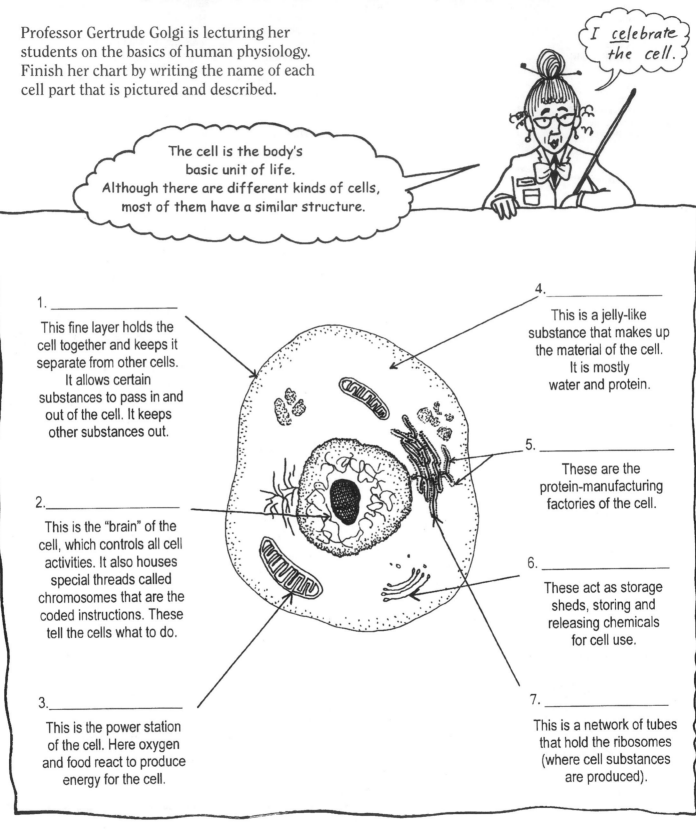

1. _____

This fine layer holds the
cell together and keeps it
separate from other cells.
It allows certain
substances to pass in and
out of the cell. It keeps
other substances out.

2. _____

This is the "brain" of the
cell, which controls all cell
activities. It also houses
special threads called
chromosomes that are the
coded instructions. These
tell the cells what to do.

3. _____

This is the power station
of the cell. Here oxygen
and food react to produce
energy for the cell.

4. _____

This is a jelly-like
substance that makes up
the material of the cell.
It is mostly
water and protein.

5. _____

These are the
protein-manufacturing
factories of the cell.

6. _____

These act as storage
sheds, storing and
releasing chemicals
for cell use.

7. _____

This is a network of tubes
that hold the ribosomes
(where cell substances
are produced).

Use with page 15.

Name _____

# GETTING COMPLICATED

The structures that make up human bodies start out simple and get complicated quickly. Identify these different cell types. Label each with one of these: bone, blood, nerve, sperm, muscle.

Every body has more than 50 billion **cells**. 1

Cells group together to form **tissues**. 2

Different kinds of tissues group together to form **organs**. Each organ has a special job in the body. 3

Organs that have closely-related jobs work together in **systems**. 4

1._____

2._____    3._____

4._____    5._____

Name the 4 kinds of tissue in the human body.

6. _____    8. _____

7. _____    9. _____

Name 10 organs in the human body.

10. _____    15. _____

11. _____    16. _____

12. _____    17. _____

13. _____    18. _____

14. _____    19. _____

Name 5 different body systems.

20. _____    22. _____

21. _____    23. _____

24. _____

Use with page 14.

Name _____

# SORTING OUT SYSTEMS

Dr. Scapula works in the research section of the hospital where different body systems are studied. Each system is studied on a different floor of the building. The elevator will take the doctor to the floor of her choice. Write the number of the correct floor for each of the questions. (There may be more than one correct answer to some questions, and a floor may be used more than once as an answer.)

Which floor will Professor Scapula visit to investigate . . .

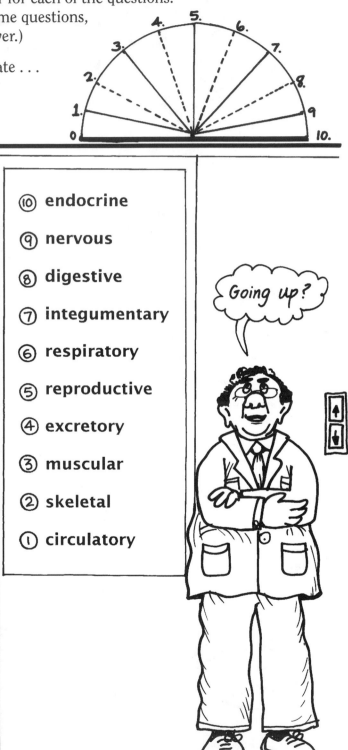

_____ A. ways that the body changes food to a form that is usable by all its cells?

_____ B. organs and structures that cover and protect the body?

_____ C. ways the body gets rid of its waste products?

_____ D. a system that gives shape and strength to the body?

_____ E. a system that enables the body to move?

_____ F. a system that enables people to produce offspring?

_____ G. how the body transports blood, nutrients, and other materials through a system of vessels?

_____ H. the system designed to carry messages between the brain and the rest of the body?

_____ I. how the body produces the hormones and chemicals that control many of its functions?

_____ J. a system that supplies oxygen to the cells and removes carbon dioxide from the blood?

_____ K. the system that controls muscles and regulates body activities?

_____ L. the system that supports and shapes the body and protects its internal organs?

⑩ **endocrine**

⑨ **nervous**

⑧ **digestive**

⑦ **integumentary**

⑥ **respiratory**

⑤ **reproductive**

④ **excretory**

③ **muscular**

② **skeletal**

① **circulatory**

Use with page 17.

Name

*Basic Skills/Human Body & Health 6-8+*

# GET ORGAN-IZED!

Nurse Constance Kare is escorting a patient for a treatment. She needs to understand the different body systems in order to get the patient to the right department in the hospital. Help her understand which organs belong to which systems. (Circle one answer for each question.)

### Where would you find . . .

1. a **thyroid gland**?
   a. in the digestive system
   b. in the integumentary system
   c. in the endocrine system
   d. in the circulatory system

2. **phalanges**?
   a. in the reproductive system
   b. in the respiratory system
   c. in the excretory system
   d. in the skeletal system

3. a **gall bladder**?
   a. in the nervous system
   b. in the integumentary system
   c. in the digestive system
   d. in the circulatory system

4. an **axon**?
   a. in the respiratory system
   b. in the reproductive system
   c. in the circulatory system
   d. in the nervous system

5. a **ventricle**?
   a. in integumentary system
   b. in the circulatory system
   c. in the excretory system
   d. in the endocrine system

6. a **Fallopian tube**?
   a. in the reproductive system
   b. in the muscular system
   c. in the skeletal system
   d. in the digestive system

7. a **duodenum**?
   a. in the digestive system
   b. in the nervous system
   c. in the reproductive system
   d. in the circulatory system

### Which is NOT in . . .

8. the **endocrine system**?
   a. diaphragm      c. adrenal gland
   b. parathyroid    d. pineal gland

9. the **digestive system**?
   a. liver          c. small intestine
   b. esophagus      d. Eustachian tube

10. the **respiratory system**?
    a. bronchiole   c. trachea
    b. stirrup      d. lungs

11. the **skeletal system**?
    a. ulna         c. patella
    b. testes       d. clavicle

12. the **circulatory system**?
    a. platelets    c. pancreas
    b. vena cava    d. atrium

13. the **integumentary system**?
    a. blood cells  c. hair
    b. skin         d. fingernails

14. the **nervous system**?
    a. dendrites    c. radius
    b. ganglia      d. spinal cord

15. the **excretory system**?
    a. kidneys      c. urethra
    b. skin         d. ligaments

16. the **muscle system**?
    a. deltoids     c. quadriceps
    b. pelvis       d. triceps

17. a **reproductive system**?
    a. uterus       c. urethra
    b. cervix       d. bladder

Use with page 16.

Name

# KNOW YOUR BONES

Do you know these bones? Students of medicine need to know these and the many other bones in the body. They study a model and ask questions to learn about bones. Answer these questions. Then use the skeleton to help you complete the chart for the Broken Bones Clinic on the next page (page 19).

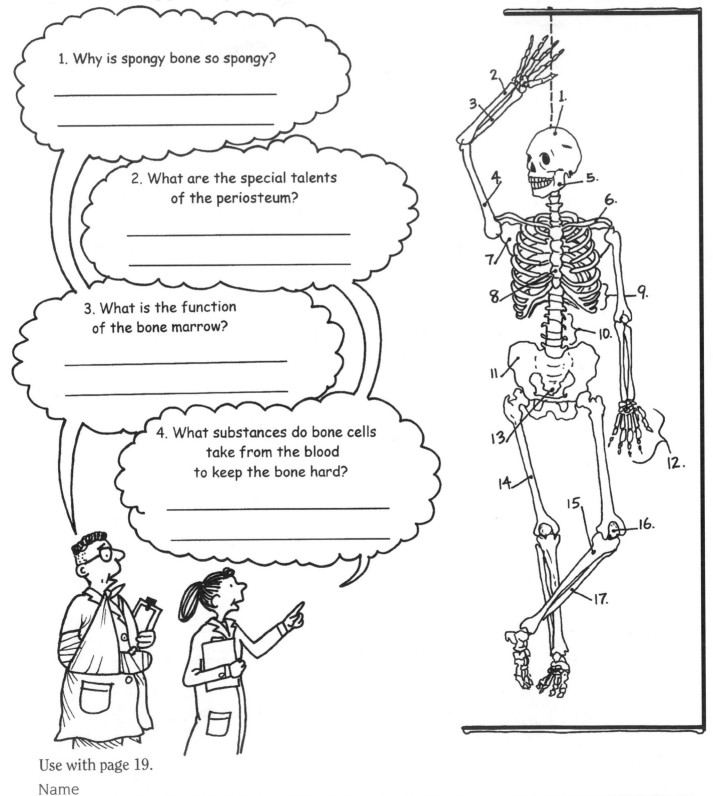

1. Why is spongy bone so spongy?

_____

_____

2. What are the special talents of the periosteum?

_____

_____

3. What is the function of the bone marrow?

_____

_____

4. What substances do bone cells take from the blood to keep the bone hard?

_____

_____

Use with page 19.

Name _____

The doctors at the Broken Bones Clinic see every kind of broken bone. They keep track of which bones each patient has broken. Finish this week's chart. Write the name of the bone for each description. Then write the number of that bone as shown on the page 18 diagram.

**BROKEN BONES CLINIC**

## BROKEN BONES (Week of March 5 – 11)

### Description of the Break

| Date | Patient Name | Description of the Break | Bone Name | Number |
|------|------|------|------|------|
| 3/5 | A. Freddy | fracture in the upper arm bone | | |
| 3/5 | B. Neddy | fractures in six finger bones | | |
| 3/6 | C. Betty | two breaks in the lower inside arm bone | | |
| 3/6 | D. Teddy | crack in the knee bone | | |
| 3/7 | E. Billy | compound fracture in the upper leg bone | | |
| 3/8 | F. Millie | cracks in each of the three bones that form a bow-like structure to support and protect the internal organs of the lower abdomen | | |
| 3/8 | G. Willie | crack in the skull bone | | |
| 3/9 | H. Winnie | fracture in the smaller of the lower leg bones | | |
| 3/9 | I. Ginny | cracks in eight of the bones which are part of the expanding bone framework that encloses the chest, protecting major internal organs | | |
| 3/9 | J. Vinnie | crack in the shoulder blade | | |
| 3/9 | K. Lester | crack in the tailbone | | |
| 3/10 | L. Chester | fracture in the outside lower arm bone | | |
| 3/10 | M. Dusty | fracture in the collar bone | | |
| 3/11 | N. Rusty | crack in the shin bone | | |
| 3/11 | O. Andy | crack in the breast bone | | |
| 3/11 | P. Randy | crack in 3 of the bones that make up the spinal column | | |
| 3/11 | Q. Sandy | crack in the jaw bone | | |

Use with page 18.

Name

# A MATTER OF MOVEMENT

Dr. Sara Bellum begins her day in the hospital gym doing a morning workout. She could not do these exercises if her body could not bend. This bending is made possible by certain body structures. Answer these questions about some of the movements that are a part of her workout.

1. What structures allow Dr. Bellum's body to bend at places such as the knees, spine, elbows, and neck?

_____

2. What strong, flexible fibers hold her bones together and stretch to allow bending?

_____

3. Pads of rubbery protein cushion the movable joints at the ends of many of her bones. What are these pads?

_____

4. What kind of joint allows Sara to bend her knees while she does knee bends? _____

5. What kind of joint allows Sara to do head circles? _____

6. What kind of joint allows her to do arm circles? _____

7. What kind of joint allows her spine to bend as she stretches toward the floor? _____

8. Last year Sara stretched an ankle ligament beyond its limit while exercising. This caused an injury to her ankle. What is this kind of injury called? _____

Look at the examples of the different kinds of joints.
Name the kind of joint shown: *fixed, sliding, ball & socket, pivot,* or *hinge*

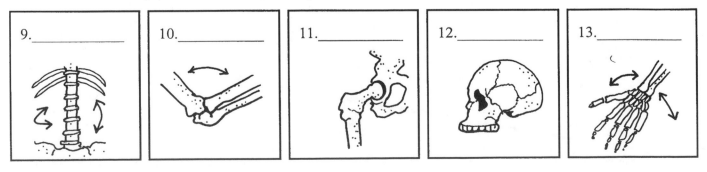

9._____   10._____   11._____   12._____   13._____

Name _____

# A MATTER OF MUSCLE

Reginald is recovering from a bad accident. After lying in bed for weeks, his muscles have become weak. He needs regular physical therapy and exercise to rebuild his strength. Answer these questions about his body's activities during his physical therapy session.

1. When Reginald starts doing the pull-ups (using his arms to pull his chin up to a bar), which muscle group is LEAST likely to be strengthened?
   a. trapezius        d. quadriceps
   b. pectorals        e. biceps
   c. triceps          f. deltoids

2. When his arms bend to pull his body up, which muscle group will contract?
   a. the biceps        b. the triceps

3. When Reginald bends his arm to lift a heavy barbell toward his chest, which muscle group will relax?
   a. the biceps        b. the triceps

4. While he exercises his lower body on the stair-stepper, what muscles is Reginald using?
   a. gastrocnemius     c. hamstrings     e. satori
   b. deltoids          d. quadriceps     f. gluteus maximus

5. When Reginald bends his knee to push on the step, which muscle group will relax?
   a. the hamstrings     b. the quadriceps

6. When his quadriceps bulge out, are these muscles contracting or relaxing?

   _____

7. What joins his muscles to his bones? _____

Name the three different kinds of muscles:

8. _____ muscle, found in arteries and walls of the digestive system, moves in slow, automatic contractions.

9. _____ muscle, found only in the heart, moves with strong automatic contractions.

10. _____ muscle, using powerful contractions, performs body movements.

Name _____

# A BRAINY PUZZLER

Neurologist, Dr. Nellie Neuron, has designed a puzzle to sharpen her students' knowledge about the nervous system. Use your brain cells and your understanding of the nervous system to solve her puzzle. The clues for the puzzle are found on the next page (page 23).

Use with page 23.

Name

Use the clues to solve the "brainy puzzle" on page 22.

# CLUES

## Across

2. the nervous system made up of nerves outside the brain and spinal cord

4. a long nerve fiber that carries impulses from one nerve cell to the next

5. the space between neurons

7. the branch of a nerve cell that receives stimuli

10. part of the brain that controls balance

12. the largest part of the brain; controls thinking and memory

13. neurons that carry impulses from receptors to the central nervous system

14. neurons that carry impulses away from the central nervous system to the body parts that react (such as muscles)

16. small groups of nerves outside the brain and spinal cord

18. the system of nerves that work automatically

## Down

1. thick cord of nerves that runs from the brain down through the column of vertebrae

3. connecting nerve cells

6. response to a stimulus that does not involve the brain

8. a nerve message

9. a nerve cell

11. part of the brain at the base of the skull; controls breathing, heartbeat, and reflexes

12. the nervous system made up of the brain and the spinal cord

14. fatty layer that encloses some axons, helping to speed up the passage of messages along the nerve

15. the side of the brain responsible for imagination

17. the side of the brain responsible for logical thinking

During Dr. Neuron's class, one of the students was stung by a yellow jacket. Briefly explain the nerve activities that led the student to respond by brushing away the bee from her arm.

Use with page 22.

Name

# THE EYES HAVE IT

In the Eye Clinic, Nurse Victor V. Ishun gives an eye exam to 5-year old Sam.
Finish the description of the way Sam's eyes see the elephant on the chart.

Like everything else Sam sees, the elephant picture reflects rays of light. The light rays bounce off the picture and travel to Sam's eyes. The light enters each eye by first traveling through the thin, transparent protective layer over the eye. This layer is the [1]_____, Next, the light passes through a tougher outer protective layer called the [2] _____. Although it is transparent at the front of the eye, this is part of the whole layer that Sam thinks of as the "whites" of his eye. The proper name for the "whites" of the eye is the [3] _____. Next, the light rays enter further into the eye through the [4] _____, a small hole at the center. The colored part of the eye, the [5] _____, is muscular and can change the size of the hole to let more or less light inside.

Next, the light carrying the image passes through the [6] _____, a transparent disc which helps to focus the image by bending the light just the right amount. The light goes on through the center of the eye, passing through clear fluids called [7] _____. The image is projected onto the [8] _____, a layer in the back of the eye which is made up of millions of light-sensitive receptors. By the time the light gets to this area, it has been bent so that the image is upside down. The [9] _____ carries this image, in the form of impulses, along to the brain. The brain is able to interpret the image right side up.

Sam's eye has some other important features. The [10] _____ can close to cover and protect his eyes. Every time they close, they wash [11] _____ over the eyes to keep them clean. Sam's [12] _____ keep specks of dust and dirt out of his eyes. Six [13] _____ attached to each eye control and coordinate the movements of the eye. Many blood cells bring food and oxygen to his eyes in a layer called the [14] _____.

Name _____

# MUSIC TO THE EARS

At night, Patricia Pitch mops the floors in the hospital halls. Tonight she is listening to some great jazz music on her CD player as she works.

Identify the parts of her ear that make it possible for her to hear this music. Write the letter from the diagram for each structure. Then write the name of the structure.

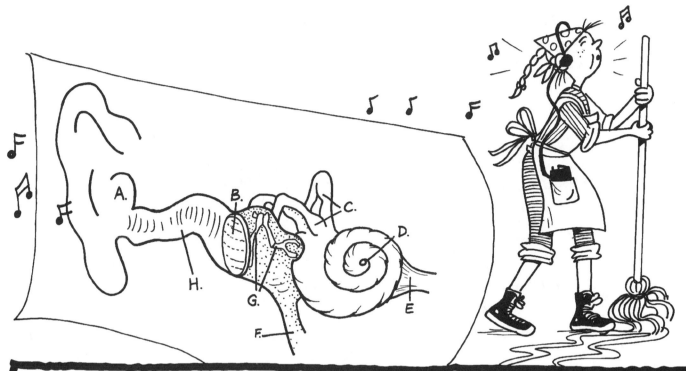

| Ear Structure | Name | Letter |
|---|---|---|
| This tightly-stretched membrane separates Patricia's outer ear from the inner ear. It vibrates when sound hits it. | 1. | |
| This fluid-filled, coiled tube contains nerve endings that pick up vibrations from the sound. The fluid vibrates hair cells, which pass a signal to the nerve that carries the impulses on to the brain. | 2. | |
| This carries the impulses from the receptor cells in the cochlea to her brain. | 3. | |
| This funnel-shaped structure directs the sound into Patricia's ear. | 4. | |
| This passageway from the back of the nose allows air to pass into her middle ear. This is important, because it allows the air pressure on both sides of her eardrum to remain equal. | 5. | |
| These canals contain fluid and nerve cells. The nerve cells are very sensitive to movement, and help Patricia keep her balance. | 6. | |
| This tube is lined with hairs and produces wax. The sound waves carrying the music pass through this tube toward the ear drum. | 7. | |
| These tiny bones pass the music vibrations from the eardrum on to Patricia's inner ear. *(Name all three.)* | 8. | |

Name _____

# ABOUT THAT HOSPITAL FOOD . . .

The patients on Floor 12 spend a lot of time discussing the hospital food. They have strong opinions about its taste, smell, and appearance. Bud deSalva, a patient on this floor, can smell the food even before it arrives by his bedside. His mouth starts salivating when he hears the food cart in the hall!

Today, the patients have been asked to complete a questionnaire about the hospital food. Bud has answered the easy questions. Answer the questions he has not finished. These may take some research.

## FOOD QUESTIONNAIRE- Body-Wise Medical Center

Date: _7/5_

Name _Bud de Salva_

Room # _1223_

1. How would you rate the taste of the meals you've been served at the medical center?
   a. superb    b. very good    c. just okay    d. not great    e. inedible

2. How would you rate the smell of the food?
   a. extremely appealing    b. average    c. worse than average    d. terrible

3. How would you rate the food's preparation and appearance?
   a. appealing    b. somewhat appealing    c. average    d. poor    e. very unappealing

4. What suggestions do you have for the food? _more milkshakes and pizza_

5. What special cells allow you to smell the hospital food? _____

6. How do these cells work to make smell possible? _____

7. How do taste buds make it possible for you to taste your food? _____

8. About how many taste buds do you have? _____

9. How does saliva play a part in tasting food? _____

10. What part of the tongue tastes the sweet jello? _____

11. What part of the tongue tastes the salty ham? _____

12. What part of the tongue tastes the bitter black tea? _____

13. What part of the tongue tastes the sour pickles? _____

14. What area of the brain interprets smells? _____

Name _____

# A TOUCHING EXPERIENCE

The sensitivity of skin is something that Lester Lesion knows all too well these days. Lester spent a week on a difficult mountain bike adventure. It was so bad that he ended up with terrible, blistering sunburn. But worse, Lester took a monumental spill on his bike and slid several feet on a gravel road. The doctor is explaining some things to Lester about his skin.

**Fill in the missing words from the doctor's comments. Use the words below.**

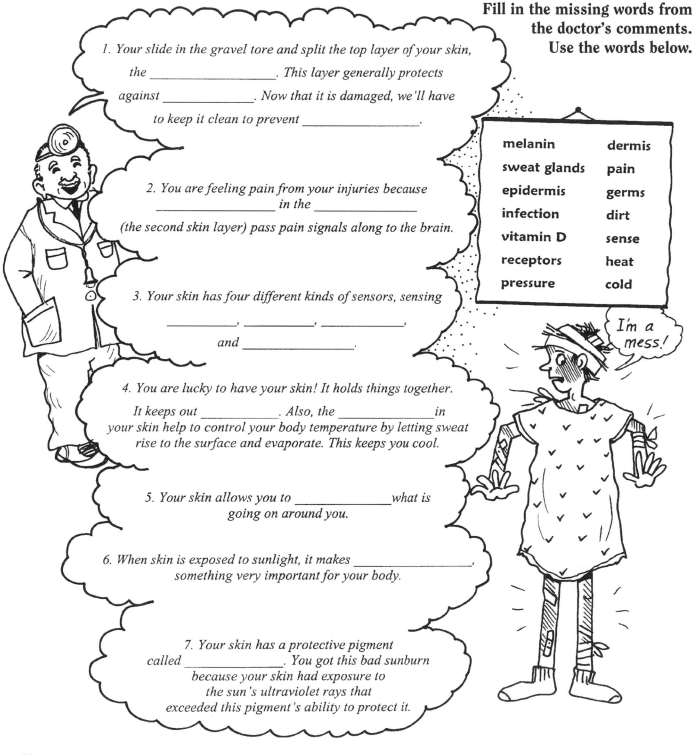

1. Your slide in the gravel tore and split the top layer of your skin, the _____. This layer generally protects against _____. Now that it is damaged, we'll have to keep it clean to prevent _____.

2. You are feeling pain from your injuries because _____ in the _____ (the second skin layer) pass pain signals along to the brain.

3. Your skin has four different kinds of sensors, sensing _____, _____, _____, and _____.

4. You are lucky to have your skin! It holds things together. It keeps out _____. Also, the _____ in your skin help to control your body temperature by letting sweat rise to the surface and evaporate. This keeps you cool.

5. Your skin allows you to _____ what is going on around you.

6. When skin is exposed to sunlight, it makes _____, something very important for your body.

7. Your skin has a protective pigment called _____. You got this bad sunburn because your skin had exposure to the sun's ultraviolet rays that exceeded this pigment's ability to protect it.

| | |
|---|---|
| melanin | dermis |
| sweat glands | pain |
| epidermis | germs |
| infection | dirt |
| vitamin D | sense |
| receptors | heat |
| pressure | cold |

I'm a mess!

Name _____

*Basic Skills/Human Body & Health 6-8+*

# BLOOD REALLY GETS AROUND

Herman Globin has stopped in at the clinic to donate blood. While waiting for his blood to be taken, he talks loudly to the donor next to him. Herman is sure he knows all the facts about blood and circulation.

*BLOOD BANK WAITING ROOM*

*I know everything. Let me tell you···*

How much does he really know? Read his statements. Circle the number if the statement is correct. If it is wrong, cross out the wrong words and write words to make the statement correct.

1. A person with type B blood can safely receive blood only from a type AB or a type B.

2. White blood cells can pass through the walls of your blood vessels into other tissues.

3. Plasma is a part of blood that carries digested food substances and waste products.

4. A donor with blood type AB can give blood to someone with any other blood type.

5. The disease fighters in your blood that make antibodies are white blood cells.

6. Your veins are red because they have hemoglobin, which carries oxygen.

7. There are many more white blood cells than red blood cells in your body.

8. The tiny pieces of cells that help your blood clot are called platelets.

9. Your arteries have valves to prevent the blood from flowing backwards.

10. Your arteries are blue, because they carry blood with wastes.

11. The blood flows at a higher pressure in veins than in arteries.

12. You have thousands of miles of blood vessels in your body.

13. The walls in arteries are thicker than the walls in veins.

14. Blood travels around your body in tubes called vessels.

15. Blood is made up of different cells floating in plasma.

16. The main artery in the body is the carotid artery.

17. The main vein in your body is the vena cava.

18. All your blood cells are made in your liver.

19. The walls of capillaries are one cell thick.

20. The aorta carries blood to the brain.

*No one told me that there would be a needle involved!*

Use with page 29.

Name _____

# A "HEART"-Y INVESTIGATION

At the end of her workout, Nurse Paula Monnary stops to check her pulse. She finds that her heart rate is 138. Do some "hearty" research to find out some facts about Paula's heart structure and functions.

1. What causes Paula to have a pulse?

   _____

2. What is a heart rate?

   _____

3. What causes the sound of Paula's heartbeat?

   _____

4. Give a general explanation of the way Paula's heart works to circulate blood around her body. Use the diagram, the letters from the diagram, and the following words as a part of your explanation.

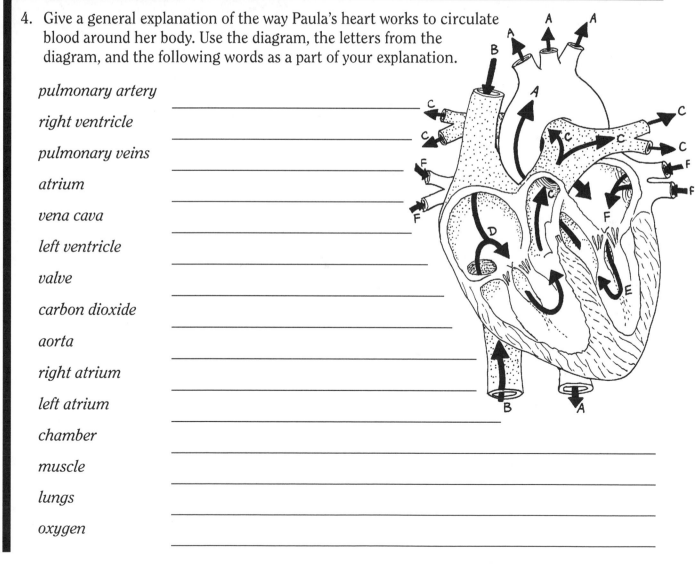

*pulmonary artery* _____

*right ventricle* _____

*pulmonary veins* _____

*atrium* _____

*vena cava* _____

*left ventricle* _____

*valve* _____

*carbon dioxide* _____

*aorta* _____

*right atrium* _____

*left atrium* _____

*chamber* _____

*muscle* _____

*lungs* _____

*oxygen* _____

Name _____

# EASY BREATHING

The entire staff in the obstetrical unit is celebrating the birth of triplets. They are blowing up balloons to decorate the nursery. It's a good thing there are some healthy respiratory systems in the group!

Since they've got 100 balloons, they'll need to do a lot of breathing in and out for this task.

Label the body structures that are used in the breathing process.

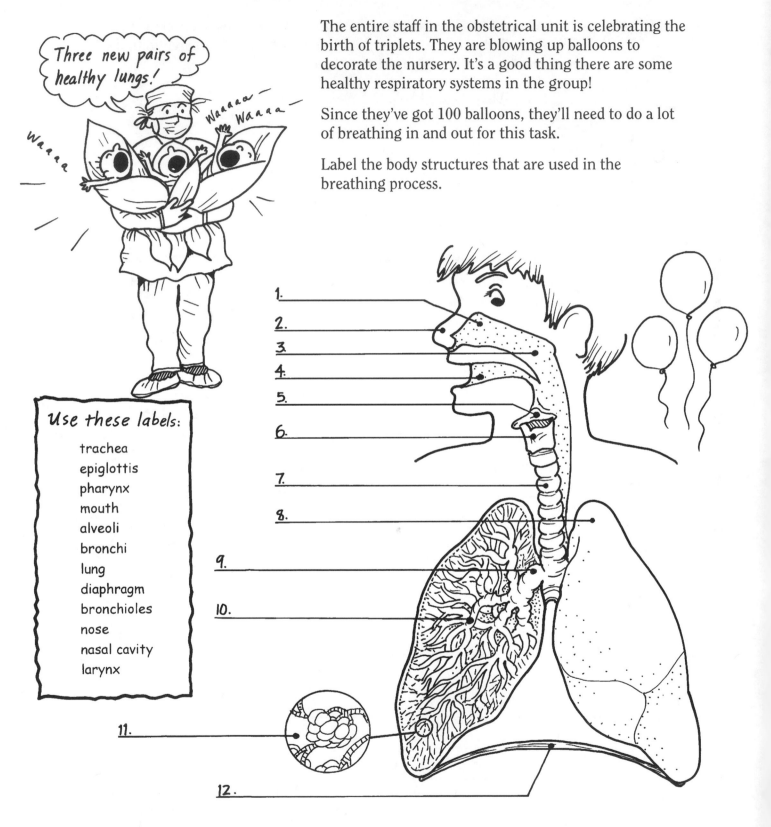

Three new pairs of healthy lungs!

Use these labels:

  trachea
  epiglottis
  pharynx
  mouth
  alveoli
  bronchi
  lung
  diaphragm
  bronchioles
  nose
  nasal cavity
  larynx

1.
2.
3.
4.
5.
6.
7.
8.
9.
10.
11.
12.

Use with page 31.

Name

Answer the questions to describe how the respiratory system of Nurse Rex Hale is functioning as he breathes in and out to blow up balloons.

# ═══ BREATHING IN ═══

1. What do the hairs in his nose and the mucus in his nose and throat accomplish when he inhales?

   _____

2. Where does air travel after it is taken into his mouth? _____

3. What happens to his ribs when he inhales? _____

4. What does his diaphragm do when he inhales? _____

5. What happens to the volume of his chest cavity when he inhales? _____

6. How does oxygen that he breathes in with the air get into his blood? _____

7. What does his epiglottis do when he inhales? _____

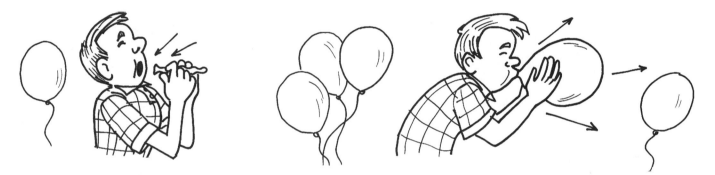

# ═══ BREATHING OUT ═══

8. How does the carbon dioxide get out of the bloodstream back into his lungs to be breathed out?

   _____

9. What path does the air with wastes follow to leave his body? _____

   _____

10. What happens to his ribs when he exhales? _____

11. What does his diaphragm do when he exhales? _____

12. What happens to the volume of his chest cavity when he inhales? _____

   _____

Use with page 30.

Name _____

# ONCE UPON A SWALLOW

When Bertha Byal took a huge bite of a delicious burrito, she had no idea that she was eating something other than the soft gooey cheese, beans, and tortilla. A large safety pin had fallen off the cook's apron and was wrapped up in her burrito. When she realized her predicament, she rushed to the hospital with the pin stuck somewhere in her digestive system.

Where was the pin? At the hospital, doctors probed, poked, and X-rayed the organs and structures that are part of her digestive system looking for the pin.

First, label the parts of the digestive system shown on the doctor's chart. Then, follow along with the doctors as they hunt for the pin. As each place they search is described (on page 33), write the name of the organ or structure.

Label these structures:

| | |
|---|---|
| ____ pharynx | ____ gallbladder |
| ____ teeth | ____ stomach |
| ____ large intestine | ____ pancreas |
| ____ tongue | ____ rectum |
| ____ liver | ____ esophagus |
| ____ salivary glands | ____ duodenum |
| | ____ small intestine |

Use with page 33.

Name

The doctors searched to see if they could find the pin stuck in any of these places. Write the name of the organ or structure (*not all of these structures are shown in the diagram on page 32*).

_____ 1. Was the pin stuck in the flap that closes when Bertha swallows to block off her trachea so food does not go down toward her lungs?

_____ 2. Did the pin lodge itself between the structures that break up food into small parts and mix it with saliva for easier swallowing?

_____ 3. Could the pin still be in the muscular tube that squeezes food along toward the stomach by peristalsis?

_____ 4. The doctors wondered if the pin was hiding underneath the organ whose muscles move food to force it back into the pharynx.

_____ 5. Could the pin be stuck in the organ that makes bile to help break up fats?

_____ 6. Is it somewhere in that amazingly long, winding organ where food is in a form so that it can pass through the walls of the organ into the blood?

_____ 7. Might the pin have gone no further than the opening at the back of the throat?

_____ 8. Did the pin perhaps lodge itself in one of the organs that make juices to aid in the initial mixing with food and breaking it down into particles?

_____ 9. Maybe the pin is somehow caught in the organ that stores bile until it is needed for digestion.

_____ 10. Could the pin be hiding among the millions of tiny finger-like projections where nutrients pass through the membranes to enter the blood or lymph vessels?

_____ 11. Hopefully the pin did not puncture the organ that makes insulin and other enzymes to help break up food in the small intestine!

_____ 12. Is it perhaps stuck in the wall of the organ that takes most of the water out of the food that cannot be digested?

_____ 13. Was the pin, perhaps, lodged inside the organ where food is churned around, and where hydrochloric acid digests proteins and kills bacteria?

_____ 14. Could the pin have made it all the way to the end of the large intestine to the place where solid wastes pass out of the body?

_____ 15. They've spotted it! It has worked its way into the first part of the small intestine where bile and other enzymes mix with the food as it comes out of the stomach.

Now that we've found it — how do we get it out?

X-RAY

Use with page 32.

Name _____

# GLAND ALERT

In the Endocrinology Lab, lab technician G.G. Land is keeping a record of the patients and their ailments. Her notebook describes difficulties or symptoms that have brought each patient's file to the lab. Read each description in the notebook. Write the name of the gland that is likely to be involved with the problem. Answers may be used more than once.

| Patient | Symptoms | Gland | Patient | Symptoms | Gland |
|---|---|---|---|---|---|
| 1. J. Slow | trouble with control of all other glands | | 7. B. Nee | problem with rate of bone growth | |
| 2. R. Pitt | immune system not rejecting germs | | 8. L. Bow | amount of calcium in blood and bones out of control | |
| 3. C. Brayne | problem with control of sugar metabolism | | 9. N. Trist | adrenalin levels stay very high even when not frightened or angry | |
| 4. B. Legg | body temperature, hunger, and thirst out of control | | 10. T. Shugg | problem with production of eggs | |
| 5. M. Groe | problem with the kidneys' production of urine | | 11. K. Bone | trouble with salt and water balance | |
| 6. J. Foote | rate at which food is turned into energy is too high | | 12. B. Blance | problem with production of sperm cells | |

Name

# WHAT A WASTE!

The garbage collectors spend most of the night carrying away the waste of the medical center; some of the waste is quite interesting. Tonight they have found a discarded study sheet about waste.

The student who wrote the notes apparently was doing research or studying for a test. How much of the information has this student recorded correctly?

Look for any errors in the student's notes.
Cross out or add any organs to the sheet to make it correct.

## WASTE SYSTEMS
### The Body's Excretory Organs

| Waste-Removal Function | Names of organs that perform the function |
|---|---|
| 1. Remove water from the body | kidneys, bladder, ureter |
| 2. Remove carbon dioxide from the body | lungs, liver |
| 3. Remove body heat | lungs |
| 4. Filter toxic substances out of the blood | gall bladder |
| 5. Remove salt from the body | skin |
| 6. Carry urine to bladder | small intestine |
| 7. Carry urine out of bladder | Eustachian tube |
| 8. Store urine before it is passed out of the body | pancreas |
| 9. Remove chemical wastes from the blood | kidneys, liver |

10. How does the skin function as a waste-removal organ?

_____

_____

_____

Name _____

# IT TAKES TWO

It takes two human reproductive cells joining together for human reproduction to take place. Nervously waiting in the lounge outside the hospital delivery room, Charlie pages through a book about the reproductive system. Some parts of the text are missing from the book. Supply the missing information.

Write the missing labels onto each diagram. Then write the missing description of the process of fertilization.

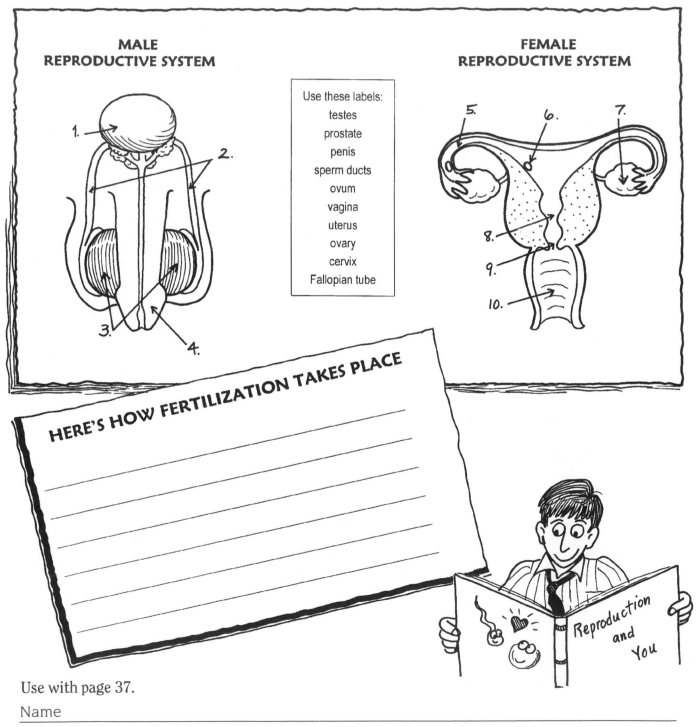

**MALE REPRODUCTIVE SYSTEM**

**FEMALE REPRODUCTIVE SYSTEM**

Use these labels:

testes
prostate
penis
sperm ducts
ovum
vagina
uterus
ovary
cervix
Fallopian tube

HERE'S HOW FERTILIZATION TAKES PLACE

Use with page 37.

Name

There is more information missing about the reproductive system and process. Complete these sentences.

1. The eggs (ova) are stored in the _____.

2. The process in which an ovum is released is _____.

3. After an egg is released, it is drawn into one of the _____.

4. The egg passes into the _____, a hollow organ with muscular walls.

5. Sperm are made in _____.

6. Sperm swims in a fluid called _____.

7. Sperm travels from its origin to the penis through tubes called_____.

8. The function of sperm is _____.

9. Fertilization of eggs by sperm takes place in the _____.

10. If an egg is fertilized, it may implant itself in _____.

11. If an egg is not fertilized, it _____.

12. The uterus gets ready to nurture a fertilized egg by_____.

13. A fertilized egg begins to _____ and grows into an embryo.

14. The embryo grows into a fetus, and the fetus develops. This takes place in the _____.

15. The function of the placenta in fetal development is_____.

16. The function of the umbilical cord is_____.

17. It takes about_____(*time)* for the fetus to develop.

18. The process of preventing fertilization of eggs is called _____.

This is all about me!

Use with page 36.

Name

# DESIGNER GENES

Why do the babies in the nursery look the way they do? Why are they each different from one another? The answer has to do with their designer genes! Each of them has a unique set of genes that determine the many characteristics that make the baby an individual person, unlike others.

Track down the answers to questions about genetics and heredity to finish the Genetics Review below.

## GENETICS REVIEW

1. What is genetics?_____

2. What are genes?_____

3. What are chromosomes?_____

4. What is DNA?_____

5. How does a baby get her or his genes?_____

6. How many chromosomes will each new baby have?_____

7. What is heredity?_____

8. What is a trait?_____

9. How is a baby's sex determined?_____

10. A sperm with an X chromosome joins the ovum.  What sex will the baby be?_____

11. A sperm with a Y chromosome joins the ovum. What sex will the baby be?_____

12. How do dominant genes affect recessive genes?_____

13. Which of the following are dominant traits? *(Circle one or more.)*
    a. rounded ear lobes        b. curved little fingers        c. blonde hair
              d. dark hair            e. freckles

14. Which of the following are sex-linked traits? *(Circle one or more.)*
    a. hemophilia            b. blue eyes                c. dimples
              d. color blindness        e. tongue rolling

Use with page 39.

Name _____

While admiring the babies in the nursery, the visitors ponder some heredity questions. Write the answer to each question.

A. Cici has a colorblind father. Her mother is not colorblind and does not carry a gene for colorblindness. What are the chances that she will be colorblind?

_____

B. Casey's dad has free earlobes. His dad has attached lobes. Is Casey more likely to have free earlobes or attached lobes?

_____

C. Both of Janie's parents have dark hair. How likely is Janie to have blonde hair? (Write a fraction for the answer.)

_____

D. William has brown eyes. Is it likely that both of his parents have blue eyes?

_____

E. Angie's mom can roll her tongue. Will Angie be more likely to have that ability or more likely NOT to have that ability?

_____

F. Tad's dad has blonde hair and dimples. His mom has dark hair and no dimples. Which traits are the most likely for Tad? (Circle one.)

   a. blonde hair and dimples
   b. dark hair and dimples
   c. dark hair and no dimples
   d. blonde hair and no dimples

G. Ramon's mother is a carrier for hemophilia. Are the chances 50% or higher that Ramon will be a hemophiliac?

_____

H. Lana's mom has freckles. Her dad does not. Are the chances 50% or higher that Lana will have freckles?

_____

I. Michael's parents both have long eyelashes. His dad has a turned-up nose; his mother does not. Is Michael likely to have long eyelashes and a turned-up nose?

_____

Use with page 38.

Name _____

# DOCTOR, DOCTOR, I FEEL SICK

The emergency room is packed tonight! There is a long line of patients needing care. Read the description each patient gives of his or her ailments. Write the number of the description beside the name of the possible ailment. Use the descriptions and ailments from both pages (40–41).

1. I have an infection of my stomach and intestines.

2. Hurry, doctor! I'm suffering from an infection of my liver.

3. I have lost my voice! I have an inflammation of my voice box.

4. There is a rash breaking out all over my body. It is caused by an infectious viral disease.

5. My feet itch from a fungal infection.

6. All of my body's defenses against disease are permanently weakened.

7. There is an abnormal division of some cells and they are invading the surrounding tissues.

8. My leg is broken!

9. My muscles are so sore after I lifted a piano.

10. There is a hole in my tooth caused by decay.

11. This is a terrible disease I have. It causes lesions on my lungs.

12. My lungs are infected.

13. My gums are inflamed!

14. My trachea and bronchi are infected with bacteria, and I have this terrible, chronic cough.

15. I have a cut. It is an emergency because my blood will not clot.

16. Could this be a serious viral infection of my spinal nerve cells?

____ influenza  ____ polio  ____ strep throat  ____ athlete's foot  ____ measles  ____ mumps

____ stroke  ____ acne  ____ scarlet fever  ____ hemophilia  ____ rabies  ____ cancer

____ malaria  ____ AIDS  ____ gastroenteritis  ____ whooping cough  ____ arthritis  ____ botulism

Use with page 41.

Name _____

17. After a mosquito bit me, I got this infectious disease with terrible chills and fever.

18. I got really sick after I ate some food with a toxic germ in it.

19. My appendix is so inflamed and infected that I think it's about to burst!

20. Can you give me some medicine for all these blackheads and pimples on my skin?

21. My body is unusually sensitive to pollen. I sneeze all the time!

22. I twisted my ankle joint too far.

23. I have a bacteria-infected wound. I'm afraid I may have nerve paralysis caused by a toxin in those bacteria.

24. My parotid glands are infected.

25. A germ caused this skin infection in an oil gland.

26. The walls of my bronchi are infected.

27. I have an infected eyelid.

28. An injury to my muscle caused blood vessels to be broken.

29. My joints are swollen and sore all the time.

30. My body temperature is too high.

31. I've got this contagious skin disease spreading everywhere.

32. A dog bit me. I'm afraid I have a deadly viral disease.

Ow Ow Ow

Me, too!

EMERGENCY ROOM

Admittance Desk

____ bruise    ____ fever    ____ pneumonia    ____ tetanus    ____ cavity    ____ tuberculosis    ____ earache

____ hepatitis    ____ boil    ____ bronchitis    ____ fracture    ____ allergy    ____ appendicitis    ____ pyorrhea

____ pinkeye    ____ strain    ____ cold sore    ____ typhoid    ____ sprain    ____ impetigo    ____ laryngitis

Use with page 40.

Name

   

# AFTER-HOURS RESEARCH

Dr. Rue Bella is doing some research in the medical center library late at night after she has finished her shift. Read the titles of the books she has pulled off the shelf. Then write the letter of one book that is likely to contain information for each topic below. *(Letters may be used more than once. There may be more than one right answer for some examples.)*

Where will she read about . . .

____ 1. chemotherapy and radiation treatments?

____ 2. lead poisoning and health dangers from fluorocarbons?

____ 3. arthritis and muscular dystrophy?

____ 4. abilities of bodies to defend themselves against a disease?

____ 5. psoriasis and diabetes?

____ 6. substances that can slow or stop the growth of bacteria?

____ 7. large numbers of deaths from smallpox in the early 19th century?

____ 8. chemicals that can deaden pain or make a patient unconscious during surgery?

____ 9. pneumonia and tuberculosis?

____ 10. asthma treatments?

____ 11. Downs syndrome and hemophilia?

____ 12. treatments for stroke victims?

____ 13. chemical substances that prevent the growth of bacteria on living tissue?

____ 14. symptoms of schizophrenia?

____ 15. polio, chicken pox, and mumps?

16. Which topics will probably NOT be covered in book I? *(Circle one or more.)*

| | | |
|---|---|---|
| influenza | AIDS | athlete's foot |
| bronchitis | roseola | diabetes |
| chicken pox | cancer | psoriasis |
| allergies | mumps | malaria |

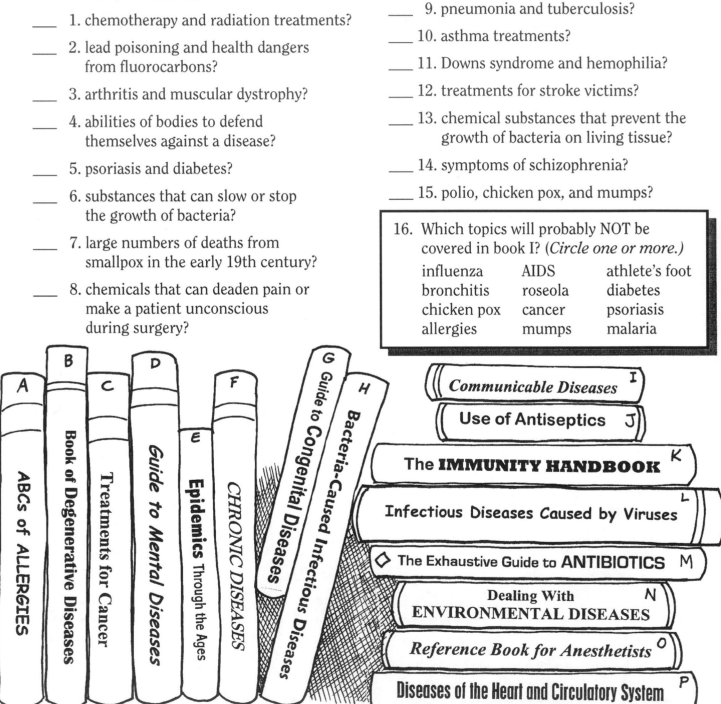

Books on shelf:
- A — ABCs of ALLERGIES
- B — Book of Degenerative Diseases
- C — Treatments for Cancer
- D — Guide to Mental Diseases
- E — Epidemics Through the Ages
- F — CHRONIC DISEASES
- G — Guide to Congenital Diseases
- H — Bacteria-Caused Infectious Diseases
- I — Communicable Diseases
- J — Use of Antiseptics
- K — The IMMUNITY HANDBOOK
- L — Infectious Diseases Caused by Viruses
- M — The Exhaustive Guide to ANTIBIOTICS
- N — Dealing With ENVIRONMENTAL DISEASES
- O — Reference Book for Anesthetists
- P — Diseases of the Heart and Circulatory System

Name _____

# WHICH TREATMENT?

When the doctors identify a patient's ailment or disease, they must move on to choose some sort of treatment. Treatments might be as simple as bandages or as complex as surgery. Choose at least one treatment, which might be used for that ailment. The treatments may be used more than once and you may identify more than one treatment for an ailment. Write the matching letter.

## TREATMENTS

A. decongestants

B. LIQUIDS

C. vaccine after getting disease

D. RADIATION

E. surgery

F. casting

G. antibiotics

H. immobilization

I. aspirin

J. antiseptics

K. REST

L. antifungal medicine

### A LONG LIST of AILMENTS

_____ 1. allergies

_____ 2. cancer

_____ 3. bacterial infection

_____ 4. dehydration

_____ 5. rabies

_____ 6. exhaustion

_____ 7. inflamed appendix

_____ 8. high fever

_____ 9. burns

_____ 10. torn ligaments

_____ 11. poison ivy

_____ 12. malaria

_____ 13. fungus

_____ 14. diseased kidney

_____ 15. heart disease

_____ 16. broken bones

_____ 17. cuts and scrapes

M. antihistamines

N. a cool bath

O. TRANSPLANT

P. chemotherapy

Q. DIALYSIS

R. physical therapy

S. MEDICINE

T. cleaning wounds

U. EXERCISE

V. change in diet

We're ready for the treatment, Doctor.

Name _____

# DISEASE-FIGHTERS

An ambulance rushes Omar to the hospital after he took a frightful fall from his trapeze. He's covered with scrapes and bruises. Some bones may be broken. There may be internal injuries.

Fortunately for Omar, his body has some natural defenses that will help prevent some further problems, and some defenses that will help him heal.

Describe the job that each of these body parts or processes does in helping the body defend against disease or heal from ailments.

> **Describe the natural reaction to a germ that enters the body.**

1. white blood cells _____

_____

2. lymph cells _____

_____

3. antibodies _____

_____

4. bone cells in the periosteum _____

_____

5. platelets in blood _____

_____

6. mucus in the nose and throat _____

_____

7. acid in the stomach _____

_____

8. clean, unbroken skin _____

_____

9. passive immunity _____

_____

10. active immunity _____

_____

Use with page 45.

Name _____

Although the body's defense system is amazing, it sometimes needs some help from outside. The patients picked up by the ambulance crew might get some help from other defense practices in the hospital. Or, they might avoid the trip to the hospital altogether, with the help of some of these practices.

Briefly describe a way that each of these practices help to defend against disease or the spread of disease.

| 11. disinfectants | 15. sunshine | 19. antiseptics |
|---|---|---|
| | | |
| 12. quarantine | 16. exercise | 20. good dental care |
| | | |
| 13. food inspection | 17. healthy eating | 21. good hygiene |
| | | |
| 14. water treatment | 18. surgery | 22. hazard avoidance |
| | | |

Use with page 44.

Name

# SMART EXERCISING

Mario M. Ussle runs the Fitness Center near the hospital. He sees to it that the visitors to the center get the three different kinds of exercise needed by their bodies. He knows that exercise helps all the parts of the body work more efficiently.

Describe the three kinds of exercise needed.

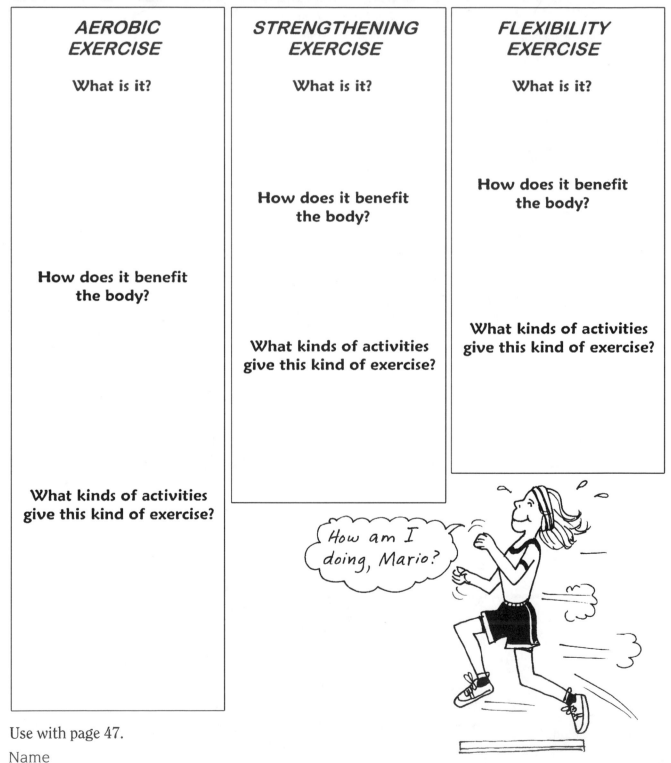

## AEROBIC EXERCISE

**What is it?**

**How does it benefit the body?**

**What kinds of activities give this kind of exercise?**

## STRENGTHENING EXERCISE

**What is it?**

**How does it benefit the body?**

**What kinds of activities give this kind of exercise?**

## FLEXIBILITY EXERCISE

**What is it?**

**How does it benefit the body?**

**What kinds of activities give this kind of exercise?**

*How am I doing, Mario?*

Use with page 47.

Name

Mario's clients are constantly asking him questions.
What answers do you think he will give to these questions?

1) **Lester Legg**: What will happen to my muscles if I don't exercise much?

1) _____

2) **Al Violli**: What happens to my heart when I exercise?

2) _____

3) **Alvin Slump**: How will bad posture affect my health?

3) _____

4) **Paula Presser**: What is isometric exercise?

4) _____

5) **Ms. A. Orta**: How does lack of exercise contribute to heart disease?

5) _____

6) **Andy McClactic**: If I exercise vigorously and stop suddenly, what will happen to my body?

6) _____

7) **Mr. N. Hale**: What happens to my lungs when I exercise?

7) _____

8) **Lou A. Chou**: How can regular exercise help me if I get pneumonia?

8) _____

*Mario's Motto: If you have your health – you have everything!*

Mario

Use with page 46.

Name _____

# SMART EATING

Leonard Tillis is the hospital's dietician. Today he has written a menu of foods and dishes for the cooks to prepare in the hospital kitchen. Use the foods on the menu to help you answer the questions.

Name one or more menu items that . . .

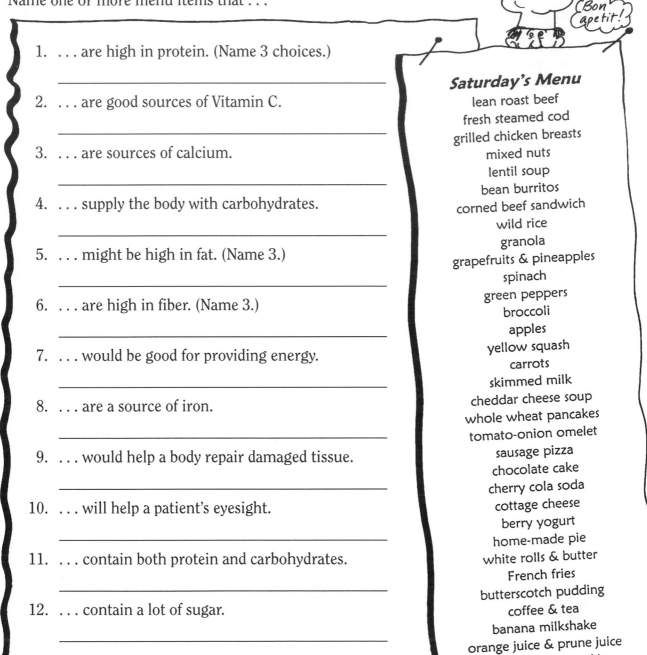

1. . . . are high in protein. (Name 3 choices.)
   _____

2. . . . are good sources of Vitamin C.
   _____

3. . . . are sources of calcium.
   _____

4. . . . supply the body with carbohydrates.
   _____

5. . . . might be high in fat. (Name 3.)
   _____

6. . . . are high in fiber. (Name 3.)
   _____

7. . . . would be good for providing energy.
   _____

8. . . . are a source of iron.
   _____

9. . . . would help a body repair damaged tissue.
   _____

10. . . . will help a patient's eyesight.
    _____

11. . . . contain both protein and carbohydrates.
    _____

12. . . . contain a lot of sugar.
    _____

**Bon apetit!**

## Saturday's Menu

lean roast beef
fresh steamed cod
grilled chicken breasts
mixed nuts
lentil soup
bean burritos
corned beef sandwich
wild rice
granola
grapefruits & pineapples
spinach
green peppers
broccoli
apples
yellow squash
carrots
skimmed milk
cheddar cheese soup
whole wheat pancakes
tomato-onion omelet
sausage pizza
chocolate cake
cherry cola soda
cottage cheese
berry yogurt
home-made pie
white rolls & butter
French fries
butterscotch pudding
coffee & tea
banana milkshake
orange juice & prune juice
lime meringue cookies

Use with page 49.

Name _____

Sometimes Leonard wants to leave personal suggestions to patients about how they can maintain or improve their nutritional health after they leave the hospital. Today he has dictated these notes for his assistant, Casey Crunch. Casey has made some mistakes, and the notes give some advice that is NOT what Leonard intended to give.

Correct any errors you find. Cross out words and write the right words to make the notes correct.

*It took me all morning to write these memos. I hope I got them right.*

**memo #1.** Mrs. Addy Pose

Make sure you eat fewer than 1200 calories a day.

**memo #2.** Hemo Globin

Your blood pressure will thank you if you avoid foods that are high in vitamins.

**memo #3.** Miss Puffy Pastry

Honey is a good source of natural protein. Use it to sweeten your baked goods and tea.

**memo #4.** Brie Edam

Limit your intake of hard cheeses and cream, since these are high in unsaturated fats.

**memo #5.** Taffy Tofu

Stay away from foods, such as yogurt, that have empty calories.

**memo #6.** Pop Cickle

Go easy on foods with complex carbohydrates (such as candy bars and soft drinks).

**memo #7.** Auntie Pasto

Simple carbohydrates are the best carbohydrates to include in your diet. You can find these in whole grain cereals and breads, and in vegetables.

**memo #8.** Tub O' Bacon

The best fats for you are those of an animal origin.

**memo #9.** Mr. Rough Stuff

It's a good idea to include very small amounts of fiber in your diet.

**memo #10.** Castor Oyll

Fish, turkey, peanut oil and olive oil are good sources of saturated fats.

Use with page 48.

Name _____

# FIRST AID ALERT

Many hospital workers and citizens of the city have come to the Medical Center for First Aid Training. The people trained in these classes put their skills to use in these incidents. Answer the questions about their first aid responses.

1. While Greg and his friend Bill were riding their bikes home in a strong windstorm, a heavy tree branch fell on Bill and knocked him off his bicycle. Greg rushed to him to check for bleeding and breathing. Are these the right things to do first?

2. Lucy has crashed into a tree on the ski hill. When the ski patrol members find her, they see that she is in shock. Should they keep her lying still with her head raised?

3. Chelsea is thrown off her horse and lands with a hard thud into a rocky, muddy creek bed. Should her friends move her to a safe, dry, warm place?

4. The Brenner's family hike was halted when a rattlesnake bit Dad. Brie insisted that they should not let Dad lie still. Is this right?

5. When John fell out of a tree, it was clear that his arm was fractured. Should his brother apply ice to John's arm?

6. B.J. is in shock after a nasty fall. Since he is conscious, his friends decide to give him liquids to drink every 15 minutes. Is this a good idea?

7. A child in Sal's neighborhood has just swallowed a large amount of bleach. Sal thinks she should keep the child from drinking any water. Is she right?

8. James has accidentally walked through a glass door. A pretty deep cut on his upper arm is bleeding badly. His friends decide to try to stop the bleeding by applying pressure to the area. They also discuss using a tourniquet. Are these good first aid practices for this injury?

9. Abbey has witnessed a horrible accident. She turns very pale and her skin gets cold and clammy. She begins to breathe unevenly and rapidly. Could she be in shock?

Use with page 51.

Name

10. Lottie ran into a wasp's nest, and she came out with several stings. Her friend Sean got busy pulling the stingers out with his fingernails. Was this a good idea?

11. Gracie is staying with her friend, Todd, while another friend goes for help. They have just found Todd lying on the sidewalk in front of his house. Should Gracie ask Todd what happened and try to get him to talk?

12. Thomas has just been stung by a wasp. Should he apply ice to the spot where the sting occurred?

13. On the way home from baseball practice, Chester runs into a barbed wire fence that he didn't see in the dark. He seems to be seriously hurt. Should his two friends immediately run to get help for Chester?

14. At a Fourth of July parade, Julio begins to look pale. He feels dizzy and has a headache. Should his friends quickly give him plenty of water and drinks of salt water every 15 minutes?

15. At the end of long, tough soccer game played in a cold wind, the coach notices that one of the team members is showing signs of hypothermia. The teammates all wrap her in a blanket and get cool water for her to drink. Is this the right response?

16. Joshua and Erwin are trying to help a friend who appears to have frostbitten fingers. They decide they should dip his fingers in hot water and get him to drink hot tea. Is this the right way to treat this?

17. While camping in a high mountainous area, Gene and some friends get caught in a snowstorm. One of his friends begins to shiver severely. His speech becomes slurred and he cannot get into his own sleeping bag. Could his friend have hypothermia?

18. Sam has a terrible nosebleed. His sister gets him to sit quietly, lean forward, and pinch his nostrils together. Is this a good idea?

19. Zeke has mistakenly swallowed kerosene. Should his friends give him syrup of ipecac so he will vomit the poison?

20. When Gina felt as if she was going to faint, her friends quickly laid her flat on the ground with her head raised up on several pillows. Was this the right thing to do for Gina?

LESSON 7:
HOW TO GIVE
ARTIFICIAL
RESPIRATION

FIRST AID DUMMY

Use with page 50.

Name

# SMART CHOICES

Everyone who graduates from the fitness course at the hospital's Fitness Center leaves with a certificate and a personal checklist of smart health choices. This checklist reminds them of smart ways to take care of their health and fitness.

Check up on your choices. How many of these smart choices do you make on a regular basis?

| ✓ | **Which SMART CHOICES do YOU make?** |
|---|---|
| | Get regular aerobic exercise for 40 minutes or more 3 or more times a week. |
| | Warm up your muscles before exercising. Cool your body down gently after exercise. |
| | Regularly do activities to keep your muscles strong. |
| | Keep your joints and muscles flexible with regular stretching. |
| | Exercise wisely and carefully to minimize the risk of injuries. |
| | Eat a balanced diet that includes lean protein sources, unsaturated fats, fiber, and healthful carbohydrates. |
| | Eat a diet with a variety of fresh foods to get enough vitamins and minerals. |
| | Drink several glasses of water a day. |
| | Include sweets, caffeine, food additives, salt, and animal fats in small amounts in your diet. |
| | Keep your skin, hair, and teeth clean. |
| | Get dental and eye checkups regularly. |
| | Pay attention to your posture when standing and sitting. Keep that backbone in correct alignment! |
| | Lift heavy things by bending your legs. Don't put unnecessary strain on your back. |
| | Get plenty of rest—8 hours a night. |
| | Pay attention to the stressors in your life. Find ways to avoid them when possible. |
| | Learn to relax. |
| | Avoid alcohol, drugs, and tobacco products. |
| | Avoid prolonged exposure to the sun without sunscreen protection |

Name

# APPENDIX

## CONTENTS

# TERMS FOR HUMAN BODY & HEALTH

adrenalin — hormone released by adrenal glands

aerobic exercise — exercise that strengthens the heart and lungs

alveoli — air-filled sacs in the lungs

antibodies — proteins made by the body that destroy poisons made by germs

aorta — largest artery in the body

arteries — vessels carrying blood away from the heart

atrium — one of two upper chambers of the heart

auditory canal — tube leading from outer to inner ear

auditory nerve — nerve that carries sound vibrations and messages to the brain

autonomic nervous system — secondary system of nerves, controls automatic processes

bile — substance produced by the liver that breaks fats down into tiny particles

bladder — organ that stores urine

bone marrow — soft tissue at center of bone

bronchi — branch tubes in the respiratory system

bronchioles — smaller tubes into the lungs

carbohydrates — energy-rich compound that comes from foods

carotid artery — artery carrying blood to the brain

cartilage — rubbery protein that cushions movable joints

central nervous system — brain and the spinal cord

cerebellum — part of the brain that controls balance and voluntary muscle action

cerebrum — largest part of the brain; controls thinking and awareness

chromosomes — threadlike structures in the cell's nucleus; carry the code that controls the cell

cochlea — spiral-shaped structure in the ear; sound waves stimulate it to produce nerve impulses

colon — the last section of the large intestine

conjunctiva — outer, thin covering of the eye

cornea — tough, protective covering of the eye

cytoplasm — the material of a cell

dermis — second layer of the skin

diaphragm — muscle that separates the chest cavity from the abdomen; assists breathing

DNA — genetic material in cell's nucleus

duodenum — tube leading out of the stomach

eardrum — tightly-stretched membrane separating outer ear from inner ear

endocrine system — network of hormone-producing glands

epidermis — protective outer layer of skin

epiglottis — flap at the top of the trachea

esophagus — tube leading from mouth to stomach

eustachian tubes — a bony tube in the ear that equalizes air pressure in the ear

excretory system — disposes of body wastes

Fallopian tubes — tubes leading from ovaries to the uterus

fertilization — process in which a male sex cell unites with a female sex cell to form a zygote

gallbladder — organ that produces bile

genes — units of inheritance passed from parents to offspring

genetics — study of heredity

heredity — passing of traits from parents to offspring

humors — fluid inside the eye

insulin — hormone that controls the amount of sugar in the bloodstream and the storage of glycogen in the liver

integumentary system — organs which cover and protect the body

iris — colored part of the eye; expands and contracts to let light into the eye

joints — place where bones join to one another

kidneys — organs that remove waste from the blood

larynx — voice box

ligaments — strong, flexible fibers that hold bones together and stretch to allow bending at joints

*A ski accident...I tripped over my own boots in the lodge.*

*Basic Skills/Human Body & Health 6-8+*

liver — the organ that cleans wastes from the blood and stores useful substances

lens — transparent disc in the eye that bends light to focus images

medulla — part of the brain that controls involuntary muscle activities; lies at the base of the skull

melanin — pigment that gives skin its color

myelin — fatty layer which encloses some axons, helping to speed up conduction of messages along the axon

nervous system — passes messages around the body

neuron — a nerve cell

optic nerve — carries messages from eyes to the brain

organ — a group of tissues that work together to perform some life activities

ovaries — female organs that produce eggs

ovum — female reproductive cell; an egg

pancreas — organ that produces insulin

parathyroids — glands that regulate the balance of calcium in the bones and blood

penis — organ of the male reproductive system

periosteum — layer of bone that grows to heal breaks

peripheral nervous system — the nerves not included in the brain or the spinal cord

peristalsis — the squeezing movement in the digestive system that moves food along

pituitary — master gland of the body; produces growth hormones

plasma — fluid in which blood cells travel

platelets — substances in blood that produce clots

proteins — organic compounds made of amino acids; important nutrients in the body

pulmonary arteries — vessels that carry oxygen-rich blood from the lungs

pupil — tiny opening in the eye that lets light in

receptors — nerve cells that receive impulses

rectum — end of the large intestine; releases solid wastes

reflex — automatic response to nerve stimuli; messages do not pass through the brain

reproductive system — system that produces offspring

respiratory system — system of organs that provides oxygen to the cells and removes waste from cells

retina — screen of light-sensitive receptions which receive images in the back of the eye

sclera — the white part of the eye

semicircular canals — canals in the ear containing fluid; help keep balance

smooth muscle — involuntary muscle present in the walls of many internal organs

sperm — male reproductive cell

sperm ducts — tubes that carry sperm into the penis

spinal cord — thick cord of nerves that runs from the brain through the vertebrae

stirrup, hammer, anvil — three bones in the inner ear that carry vibrations from sound to the auditory nerve

striated muscle — voluntary muscle made of bands called striations (also known as skeletal muscle)

system — a group of organs that work together to carry out life's activities

taste buds — groups of receptor cells in the tongue that are sensitive to chemicals dissolved in saliva

tendons — strong bands of tissue that attach the ends of muscle fibers to bones

testes — sperm-producing organ of the male reproductive system

thyroid — gland that controls the rate at which food is used in the body

tissue — groups of similar cells that specialize to do a particular job in the body

trachea — windpipe; tube carrying air to lungs

trait — a characteristic

urethra — tube that carries urine out of the body

ureters — tubes that carry urine from the kidneys to the bladder

uterus — female reproductive organ which holds a growing fetus

vagina — passageway out of the uterus

veins — vessels that carry blood to the heart

ventricle — one of two lower heart chambers

villi — small finger-like projections in the small intestine; substances pass in and out of their membranes

Books?...
Magazines?...
Dental floss?

# HUMAN BODY & HEALTH SKILLS TEST

Each correct answer is worth 1 point. Total possible points = 75

*1–12: Which body part performs these functions?*
*Write a letter from the list for each part.*

_____ 1. repairs broken bones

_____ 2. carries blood to the heart

_____ 3. controls thinking and awareness

_____ 4. carries nutrients, oxygen, and minerals in the blood

_____ 5. protects the eye

_____ 6. regulates 11 glands in the body

_____ 7. carries urine away from the bladder out of the body

_____ 8. makes antibodies

_____ 9. exchange oxygen and carbon dioxide in and out of the blood

_____ 10. helps increase the size of the chest cavity when inhaling

_____ 11. attaches muscles to bones

_____ 12. produces insulin to regulate sugar levels in the body

**Some Body Parts**
A. alveoli
B. aorta
C. bronchi
D. cerebrum
E. cornea
F. diaphragm
G. duodenum
H. epidermis
I. larynx
J. lymph cells
K. pancreas
L. periosteum
M. pituitary
N. plasma
O. retina
P. tendon
Q. trachea
R. urethra
S. vena cava

*13–23: Write an answer for each question or item.*

13. What purpose do ligaments have in the body? _____

_____

14. What is the purpose of cartilage? _____

_____

15. What kind of muscle tissue lines blood vessels? _____

16. What kind of muscle tissue is found in the heart? _____

17. What happens when muscles contract? _____

18. Give an example of a sliding joint. _____

19. What kind of a joint is shown here? _____

20. Name two joints of this kind: _____

21. Which brain part controls swallowing? _____

22. Which neurons carry impulses away from the central nervous system to muscles? _____

23. Which brain part controls balance, coordination, and muscle activity? _____

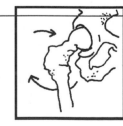

Name _____

*24–29: For each organ or body part pictured, write the name of the structure, the body system in which it functions, and a brief description of its function.*

24. **A** name _____ system _____

function _____

25. **B** name _____ system _____

function _____

26. **C** name _____ system _____

function _____

27. **D** name _____ system _____

function _____

28. **E** name _____ system _____

function _____

29. **F** name _____ system _____

function _____

*30–39: Write an answer for each question or item.*

30. How is a tissue different from an organ? _____

31. What body system produces hormones and chemicals to control functions? _____

32. What system removes toxic substances from the blood? _____

33. What determines a baby's sex? _____

34. Which organs of the body are parts of the central nervous system? _____

35. What space must impulses cross when they travel between neurons? _____

36. Which side of Max's brain is most in use when he imagines wild monsters? _____

37. How do taste buds make it possible to taste food? _____

38. How are characteristics (traits) passed from parents to offspring? _____

39.
> Both Jordan's parents have long eyelashes. His mom has blonde hair. His dad has dark brown hair. His dad can curl his tongue. His mom carries the gene for color blindness.

Which of the traits of Jordan's parents are dominant and likely to be passed on to Jordan? *(Circle one or more.)*

blonde hair      brown hair

long eyelashes      tongue curling      color blindness

Name _____

*40–49: Circle one or more answers for each.*

40. Nerve impulses are produced in response to sound waves within the ear structure called
    a. the eardrum.      b. the cochlea.      c. the semicircular canals.      d. the auditory canals.

41. Nerve endings in the skin that sense heat, cold, pressure, and pain are located in
    a. the epidermis.      b. the dermis.      c. the oil glands.      d. the fat cells.

42. Which kind of tissue would be found in the lining of the blood vessels?
    a. connective      b. epithelial      c. muscle      d. nerve

43. Freddy broke two bones in his leg. Which of these could NOT be the bones he broke?
    a. scapula      b. femur      c. tibia      d. radius      e. humerus      f. fibula      g. clavicle

44. Todd's tongue tastes bitter black tea
    a. on the front.      b. on the sides and front.      c. on the sides.      d. on the back.

45. When skin becomes sunburned, its exposure to the sun's ultraviolet rays has exceeded the protection available from the
    a. epidermis.      b. melanin.      c. sweat glands.      d. pigment.

46. A person with Type O blood can donate blood to which other blood types?
    a. none      b. A      c. B      d. AB      e. O

47. Blood flowing away from the heart is red because of the oxygen-carrying
    a. hemoglobin.      b. pigment.      c. vessels.      d. epidermis.

48. Food is absorbed into the body through the walls of the
    a. esophagus.      b. rectum.      c. stomach.      d. large intestine.      e. small intestine.

49. When Lottie bends her knee to climb a step, which will happen?
    a. The quadriceps will contract.      c. The hamstrings will relax.
    b. The hamstrings will contract.      d. The quadriceps will relax.

*50–57: Write a letter to show which disease or ailment matches the description.*

_____ 50. an infection of the lungs

_____ 51. results from abnormal insulin production

_____ 52. chronic inflammation of joints

_____ 53. a serious infection of the liver

_____ 54. inflammation of the gums

_____ 55. an environmental disease

_____ 56. a mental disease

_____ 57. abnormal division of cells that invade surrounding tissues

**BODY AILMENTS**

| | | |
|---|---|---|
| A. arthritis | J. hemophilia | S. pneumonia |
| B. asthma | K. hepatitis | T. psoriasis |
| C. bruise | L. impetigo | U. pyorrhea |
| D. bronchitis | M. lead poisoning | V. rabies |
| E. cancer | N. laryngitis | W. schizophrenia |
| F. typhoid | O. malaria | X. small pox |
| G. diabetes | P. measles | Y. strep throat |
| H. encephalitis | Q. pinkeye | Z. tetanus |
| I. fracture | R. poison ivy | |

ah choo

Name _____

58. Describe the difference between active and passive immunity: _____

_____

59. Describe the body's reaction to germs entering the body. _____

_____

*60–65: Circle one or more answers for each.*

60. Which of these would be good activities for increasing muscle flexibility?
    a. isometric exercises    b. jogging    c. rowing    d. stretching    e. yoga
    f. tennis    g. cross-country skiing    h. brisk walking    i. jumping-rope

61. Which of these activities would increase aerobic fitness?
    a. isometric exercises    b. jogging    c. rowing    d. stretching    e. yoga
    f. tennis    g. cross-country skiing    h. brisk walking    i. jumping-rope

62. To build essential amino acids needed for growth and repair of body tissue, it is important to eat
    a. fats    b. vitamins.    c. minerals.    d. proteins.    e. carbohydrates.    f. fiber.

63. In order to be used by the body as an energy source, food needs to be broken down into
    a. glucose    b. protein.    c. fats.    d. carbohydrates    e. water.

64. For which first aid emergency should you keep the victim's affected area below the heart level?
    a. stroke    b. hypothermia    c. snake bite    d. fall    e. fainting

65. For which first aid emergency should you keep the victim lying still with feet slightly elevated?
    a. burns    b. bee sting    c. fracture    d. shock    e. frostbite

*66–75: Write a letter from at least one of the foods pictured to match each description.*

_____ 66. high in protein

_____ 67. good source of Vitamin C

_____ 68. source of calcium

_____ 69. good source of fiber

_____ 70. source of carbohydrates

_____ 71. high in sugar

_____ 72. will help eyesight

_____ 73. helps repair body tissue

_____ 74. good source of iron

_____ 75. source of Vitamin D

SCORE: Total Points _____ out of a possible 100 points

Name _____

*Basic Skills/Human Body & Health 6-8+*     59    

# HUMAN BODY & HEALTH
# SKILLS TEST ANSWER KEY

1. L
2. S
3. D
4. N
5. E
6. M
7. R
8. J
9. A
10. F
11. P
12. K
13. help body bend and stretch; connect bones
14. cushion places where bones meet each other
15. smooth muscle
16. cardiac muscle
17. they thicken, tighten, do work
18. spine (Accept other examples of a sliding joint.)
19. ball & socket
20. shoulder, hip
21. medulla
22. motor neurons
23. cerebellum
24. liver; digestive; makes bile
25. nerve cell or neuron; nervous; carries impulses
26. hammer, anvil, & stirrup; sensory system or nervous system or ear; vibrate and pass vibrations along
27. kidneys; digestive or excretory; remove wastes from the body or produce urine
28. lungs; respiratory; get oxygen into body and expel carbon dioxide
29. gallbladder; digestive; store bile
30. tissue is made of specialized cells; organ is made of tissues
31. endocrine
32. digestive or excretory
33. a sperm that fertilizes the egg has either an X or Y chromosome
34. brain and spinal cord
35. synapse
36. right
37. they have receptor cells which receive stimuli from chemicals in saliva

38. chromosomes are passed to offspring from parents (carrying genes)
39. brown hair, long eyelashes, tongue curling, color blindness
40. b
41. b
42. b
43. a, d, e, g
44. d
45. b
46. b, c, d, e
47. a
48. e
49. b, d
50. S
51. G
52. A
53. K
54. U
55. M
56. W
57. E
58. Active: body makes its own antibodies to protect against disease; passive: body gets antibodies from outside source.
59. White blood cells surround and destroy germs. Lymph cells make antibodies to kill toxins from germs.
60. d, e
61. b, c, f, g, h, i
62. d
63. a
64. a
65. d
66. A, B, E, I, or L
67. C, F, G, or K
68. F of L
69. C, D, G, H, K, or N
70. C, D, G, H, K, M, N
71. K, O
72. D
73. A, B, E, F, I, L
74. A
75. B, F, L

*Basic Skills/Human Body & Health 6-8+*

# ANSWERS

## pages 10–11
1. peristalsis
2. bile
3. teeth
4. impulses, signals, or messages
5. blood
6. insulin
7. fats
8. oxygen
9. vomiting
10. pivot joint
11. cochlea; the ear
12. bile and pancreatic juices
13. the eye
14. ova or eggs
15. mucus
16. a tooth
17. water
18. digested food and waste products
19. fingernails or toenails
20. the closing of the heart valves
21. adrenalin
22. platelets

## pages 12–13
1. arteries or aorta
2. kidneys
3. periosteum
4. larynx
5. trachea
6. Eustachian tubes
7. quadriceps or muscles or ligaments
8. triceps or biceps
9. myelin
10. pancreas
11. ureters
12. cerebellum
13. diaphragm
14. parathyroid gland
15. white blood cells
16. villi
17. cartilage
18. tongue
19. retina
20. thymus
21. tendon
22. liver
23. pituitary gland
24. medulla
25. coccyx
26. epiglottis
27. marrow
28. molars or teeth
29. ovaries
30. alveoli

## page 14
1. cell membrane
2. nucleus
3. mitochondria
4. cytoplasm
5. ribosomes
6. Golgi complex
7. ER (endoplasmic reticulum)

## page 15
1. muscle
2. sperm
3. bone
4. blood
5. nerve

6–9. 4 kinds of tissue: connective tissue, epithelial tissue, muscle tissue, nerve tissue

10–19. Answers will vary. Check to see that student has named 10 different organs.

20–24. Answers will vary. Check to see that student has named 5 different body systems.

## page 16
A. 8
B. 7
C. 4 or 8
D. 2 or 3
E. 2 or 3
F. 5
G. 1
H. 9
I. 10
J. 6
K. 9 or 10
L. 2 or 3

## page 17
1. c
2. d
3. c
4. d
5. b
6. a
7. a
8. a
9. d
10. b
11. b
12. c
13. a
14. c
15. d
16. b
17. d

## pages 18–19
1. Spongy bone is spongy because its cells form a network with spaces between areas of bone. This makes the bone strong, but light.
2. The periosteum is a layer of bones that has the ability to multiply and grow to repair a break.
3. Blood cells are made in the marrow of the long bones in the body.
4. calcium and phosphorus

A. humerus—4
B. phalanges—12
C. radius—3
D. patella—16
E. femur—14
F. pelvis—11
G. cranium—1
H. fibula—17
I. ribs—9
J. scapula—7
K. coccyx—13
L. ulna—2
M. clavicle—6
N. tibia—15
O. sternum—8
P. vertebrae—10
Q. mandible—5

## page 20
1. joints or ligaments
2. ligaments
3. cartilage
4. hinge
5. pivot
6. ball & socket
7. sliding
8. sprain
9. sliding
10. hinge
11. ball & socket
12. fixed
13. pivot

## page 21
1. d
2. a
3. b
4. b
5. b
6. contracting
7. tendons
8. Smooth
9. Cardiac
10. Skeletal or Striated

## pages 22–23
*Across*
2. peripheral
4. axon
5. synapse
7. dendrite
10. cerebellum
12. cerebrum
13. sensory
14. motor
16. ganglia
18. autonomic
*Down*
1. spinal cord
3. interneurons
6. reflex
8. impulse

*Basic Skills/Human Body & Health 6-8+*     Copyright ©2002 by Incentive Publications, Inc., Nashville, TN.

9. neuron
11. medulla
12. central
14. myelin
15. right
17. left

The sting of the bee stimulates the nerve endings in the arm. The nerve endings send a message along the nerve paths to the brain, and the brain sends a message back to the hand to brush away the bee.

OR

Students might argue that the brushing away of the bee is a reflex action. In this case, the sting excites the nerves and sends an impulse (message) that causes the hand to jerk toward the arm. This response does not involve the brain.

### page 24

1. conjunctiva
2. cornea
3. sclera
4. pupil
5. iris
6. lens
7. humors
8. retina
9. optic nerve
10. eyelids
11. tears
12. eyelashes
13. muscles
14. choroid

### page 25

1. eardrum—B
2. cochlea—D
3. auditory nerve—E
4. outer ear—A
5. Eustachian tube—F
6. semicircular canals—C
7. auditory canal—H
8. hammer, anvil, stirrup—G

### page 26

Note: Answers for 6, 7, 8, 9 may vary somewhat from the answers below.
1–4. Already answered
5. olfactory cells or receptor cells
6. They are stimulated by vapors released from the food. The vapors dissolve in the mucus held by the hairs on the cells. This causes nerve impulses to be sent to the brain.
7. The taste buds are stimulated by chemicals in dissolved food. The taste buds contain receptor cells that send nerve impulses to the brain.
8. 8000-10,000
9. The saliva dissolves the food and allows chemicals to be released. The taste buds are sensitive to these chemicals.

10. front
11. front sides
12. back
13. sides
14. olfactory area

### page 27

1. epidermis, germs (or dirt), infection
2. receptors, dermis
3. pain, pressure, heat, cold
4. dirt (or germs), sweat glands
5. sense
6. vitamin D
7. melanin

### page 28

Corrected answers may vary.
1. Change *AB* to *O*.
2. correct
3. correct
4. Change *AB* to *O*.
5. correct
6. Change *veins* to *arteries*.
7. Change *white* to *red* and *red* to *white*.
8. correct
9. Change *arteries* to *veins*.
10. Change *arteries* to *veins*.
11. Change *veins* to *arteries* and *arteries* to *veins*.
12. correct
13. correct
14. correct
15. correct
16. change *carotid artery* to *aorta*.
17. correct
18. Change *liver* to *bone marrow*.
19. correct
20. Change *aorta* to *carotid artery*.

### page 29

1. the force (pressure) of the blood pushing through the arteries with each heartbeat
2. the number of times the heart beats per minute
3. the heart valves slamming shut
4. Answers will vary. See that student has written a clear, general explanation of heart function, something like this:

The superior vena cava brings low-oxygen blood (or blood full of carbon dioxide) from the body into the right atrium. (B)
The right atrium contracts and forces blood through the valve into the right ventricle. (D)
The right ventricle contracts, forcing blood through the pulmonary arteries toward the lungs. (C)
In the lungs, carbon dioxide is removed from the blood, and oxygen is put into the blood. The oxygen-rich blood flows back from the lungs through the

pulmonary veins into the left atrium. (F)
The left atrium contracts, forcing the blood through the valve into the into the left ventricle. (E)
The heart muscle pumps the blood out of the left ventricle through the aorta to the body. (A)

### page 30

1. nasal cavity
2. nose
3. pharynx
4. mouth
5. epiglottis
6. larynx
7. trachea
8. lung
9. bronchi
10. bronchioles
11. alveoli
12. diaphragm

### page 31

1. catch dirt and germs to keep them from passing into the lungs
2. through the throat, down into the trachea, into the bronchi and bronchioles to the alveoli
3. They expand or move outward.
4. It contracts (or flattens).
5. It increases.
6. It passes through the walls (membranes) of the alveoli.
7. It closes.
8. It passes through the walls (membranes) of the alveoli.
9. from the alveoli into the bronchioles, to the bronchi, trachea, and out through the mouth or nose
10. They move inward.
11. It relaxes.
12. It increases.

### page 32

A. salivary gland
B. teeth
C. tongue
D. pharynx or throat
E. esophagus
F. liver
G. stomach
H. gallbladder
I. pancreas
J. duodenum
K. large intestine
L. small intestine
M. rectum

### page 33

1. epiglottis
2. teeth
3. esophagus

4. tongue
5. liver
6. small intestine
7. pharynx
8. salivary glands
9. gallbladder
10. villi
11. pancreas
12. large intestine
13. stomach
14. rectum or anus
15. duodenum

**page 34**

1. pituitary
2. thymus
3. pancreas
4. hypothalamus or thyroid
5. pituitary
6. thyroid
7. pituitary
8. parathyroids
9. adrenals
10. ovaries
11. adrenals
12. testes

**page 35**

Answers may vary.
Organs to cross out:
1. none
2. liver
3. none
4. gallbladder
5. none
6. small intestine
7. Eustachian tube
8. pancreas
9. none

Correct organs (student should have some of these listed for each):
1. kidneys, bladder, ureter, urethra, lungs, bladder
2. lungs
3. skin, lungs
4. kidneys
5. kidneys, skin
6. ureter
7. urethra
8. bladder
9. kidneys, liver, skin
10. Perspiration removes salt and other waste products.

**page 36**

1. prostate
2. sperm ducts
3. testes
4. penis
5. Fallopian tube
6. ovum
7. ovary

8. uterus
9. cervix
10. vagina
How Fertilization Takes Place: Explanations will vary somewhat. The general process is this:

Sperm produced in the male testes travel out through the sperm ducts and out of the penis into the vagina of the female. The sperm swim up into the Fallopian tubes where they may meet an ovum. If a sperm penetrates (joins with) the ovum, fertilization will take place.

**page 37**

1. ovaries
2. ovulation
3. Fallopian tubes
4. uterus
5. the testes
6. semen
7. sperm ducts
8. to fertilize the eggs
9. Fallopian tube
10. the uterine lining
11. passes out of the vagina along with the uterine lining (menstruation)
12. thickening its lining
13. divide
14. uterus
15. protect the growing fetus
16. supply nutrients and oxygen to the fetus; carries away wastes
17. nine months
18. contraception

How Fertilization Takes Place
(Answers will vary.)
An egg is released from an ovary and travels down the fallopian tube. Sperm are released from the testes, down the sperm ducts and out through the penis. They travel into the vagina and swim up into the fallopian tubes. When one of the sperm joins with the egg, fertilization occurs.

**page 38**

Answers may vary somewhat.
1. the study of heredity
2. the unit of inheritance that carries coded instructions for traits
3. threadlike structures in the nucleus of cells that carry genes
4. genetic material in the nucleus of every cell that makes up genes and chromosomes
5. from his/her parents
6. 23 from each parent; total 46
7. the passing of traits from parents to offspring
8. a characteristic
9. by the kind of sex chromosome carried by the sperm that fertilizes the egg

10. a girl
11. a boy
12. they overrule the recessive genes
13. a, d, e
14. a, d

**page 39**

A. none
B. free
C. 1/4
D. no
E. more likely TO have the ability
F. b
G. yes
H. yes
I. yes

**pages 40–41**

1. gastroenteritis
2. hepatitis
3. laryngitis
4. measles
5. athlete's foot
6. AIDS
7. cancer
8. fracture
9. strain
10. cavity
11. tuberculosis
12. pneumonia
13. pyorrhea
14. whooping cough
15. hemophilia
16. polio
17. malaria
18. botulism
19. appendicitis
20. acne
21. allergy
22. sprain
23. tetanus
24. mumps
25. boil
26. bronchitis
27. pinkeye
28. hepatitis
29. arthritis
30. fever
31. impetigo
32. rabies

**page 42**

1. C
2. N
3. B, F, or D
4. K
5. F
6. M
7. E
8. O
9. I or H
10. A or F
11. G

12. P
13. J
14. D
15. L
16. allergies, cancer, diabetes, psoriasis

## page 43

1. A, M, or S
2. D, E, P, or S
3. G, K, or S
4. B or K
5. C
6. B or K
7. E, G, or S
8. B, G, I, N, or S
9. G, K, S, or T
10. E, K, H, R
11. S
12. K or S
13. L or S
14. E, O, Q, or S
15. E, O, S, U, or V
16. E, F, H, or R
17. J, S, or T

## pages 44–45

Answers will vary somewhat.
1. surround and digest germs
2. make antibodies to kill germs
3. kill germs
4. multiply and grow to heal breaks in bone
5. form clots to stop bleeding
6. trap germs and dust to keep them from going into lungs
7. kills germs
8. keeps dirt and germs from getting into the body
9. babies have natural passive immunity passed by their mothers-this lasts a few months
10. the body makes its own antibodies in response to a disease; when the person is exposed a second time to the disease, the body forms the same antibodies and the person does not get sick

The box at the top of page 44:
White blood cells surround and digest the germs. Lymph cells make antibodies to kill the germ.

11–22. Answers will vary. Make sure that student's answer is sensible and accurate.

## page 46

Answers will vary.

Aerobic Exercise:

*What is it?*
Aerobic exercise is exercise in which the heart works harder or beats faster for a sustained period of time.

*How does it benefit the body?*
It builds strength and stamina in the heart, and improves lung function.

*What kinds of activities give this kind of exercise?*
Many—jogging, walking, running, skipping rope, swimming, cycling, stair-stepping, cross country skiing

Strengthening Exercise:

*What is it?*
Strengthening exercise is exercise that works muscles.

*How does it benefit the body?*
It increases muscle strength and endurance.

*What kinds of activities give this kind of exercise?*
Weightlifting, rowing, canoeing, isometrics, any work or exercise that uses upper body or lower body muscle strength

Flexibility Exercise:

*What is it?*
Flexibility exercise is exercise that allows muscles to stretch and relax.

*How does it benefit the body?*
It enables the body to stretch and bend easily without injury or stiffness.

*What kinds of activities give this kind of exercise?*
Stretches

## page 47

Answers will vary.
1. They become weak and flabby.
2. Your heart works harder. It beats faster and gradually the heart muscle gets stronger.
3. It weakens some muscles and keeps others too tight. You can get problems with your back and joints.
4. Exercise that works muscles by pressing against immovable objects.
5. Fatty deposits build up in the arteries bringing blood to the heart. The heart muscle gets weaker.
6. Waste products will stay in your muscles, and your muscles will get stiff.
7. It strengthens chest muscles and increases the amount of air your lungs can hold.
8. Pneumonia puts more strain on a weak heart than on a stronger heart.

## page 48

Answers will vary. Check to see that students have at least one of the following (except for e required in 1, 5, 6)
1. roast beef, cod, chicken, nuts, lentil soup, bean burrito, sandwich, cheese soup, pizza
2. grapefruit, pineapple, orange juice, broccoli
3. milk, yogurt, cottage cheese, cheese soup, milkshake, pudding
4. rice, granola, any of the fruits or vegetables, pancakes, rolls, pizza, French fries, pudding, milkshake, orange juice, prune juice, sandwich, burrito
5. pudding, cheese soup, butter, cake, pudding, fries, milkshake, sandwich
6. rice, granola, pancakes, any fruit or vegetables
7. any of the carbohydrate items listed in # 4
8. prune juice, beef, corned beef sandwich
9. any of the proteins in # 1
10. carrots, squash, spinach, broccoli
11. sandwich, pizza, burrito, cheese soup
12. chocolate cake, soda, pudding, milkshake, lime meringue cookies

## page 49

Answers will vary.
1. Replace *fewer* with *more*.
2. Replace *high in vitamins* with *low in salt*.
3. Replace *protein* with *sugar*.
4. Replace *unsaturated* with *saturated*.
5. Replace *yogurt* with *sweets*.
6. Replace *complex* with *simple*.
7. Replace *Simple* with *Complex*.
8. Replace *best* with *worst* or replace *animal* with *vegetable*.
9. Replace *very small* with *good* or *large*.
10. Replace *saturated* with *unsaturated*.

## pages 50–51

| | | |
|---|---|---|
| 1. yes | 8. yes | 14. yes |
| 2. yes | 9. yes | 15. no |
| 3. no | 10. no | 16. no |
| 4. no | 11. yes | 17. yes |
| 5. yes | 12. yes | 18. yes |
| 6. yes | 13. no | 19. no |
| 7. no | | 20. no |

## page 52

Answers will vary.